GIVE LOVE
and Receive the Kingdom

*Essential People and Themes
of English Spirituality*

BENEDICTA WARD, SLG

PARACLETE PRESS
BREWSTER, MASSACHUSETTS

2018 First Printing

Give Love and Receive the Kingdom:
Essential People and Themes of English Spirituality

© 2018 Benedicta Ward, SLG

ISBN: 978-1-64060-097-3

The Paraclete Press name and logo (dove on cross) are trademarks of Paraclete Press, Inc.

Library of Congress Cataloging-in-Publication Data

Names: Ward, Benedicta, 1933- author.
Title: Give love and receive the kingdom : essential people and
themes of English spirituality / Benedicta Ward, SLG.
Description: Brewster, MA : Paraclete Press, Inc., 2018.
Identifiers: LCCN 2018013291 | ISBN 9781640600973 (hardcover)
Subjects: LCSH: England—Church history—449-1066. | England—
Church history—1066-1485.
Classification: LCC BR749 .W37 2018 | DDC 248.0942—dc23
LC record available at https://lccn.loc.gov/2018013291

10 9 8 7 6 5 4 3 2 1

Published by Paraclete Press
Brewster, Massachusetts
www.paracletepress.com

Printed in the United States of America

CONTENTS

* ■ *

INTRODUCTION   V

1 THE SPIRITUALITY 1
of ST. CUTHBERT

2 BEDE AND THE CONVERSION 21
of the ANGLO-SAXONS

3 BEDE 33
and THE PSALTER

4 A TRUE EASTER 79
THE SYNOD *of* WHITBY

5 ANSELM *of* CANTERBURY 101
A MONASTIC SCHOLAR

6 TWELFTH-CENTURY 127
ENGLISH HERMITS

7 FAITH SEEKING UNDERSTANDING 141
Anselm of Canterbury *and* Julian of Norwich

8 THREE PREACHERS 151
Lancelot Andrewes, Jeremy Taylor, Mark Frank

9 PILGRIMAGE OF THE HEART 169
with Special Reference to
Lancelot Andrewes *and* John Bunyan

ACKNOWLEDGEMENTS/PERMISSIONS 193

INTRODUCTION

These papers were all written for different times and occasions, and I am grateful to the editors at Paraclete Press and SLG Press for the suggestion of reprinting them under one cover. Reading them together is for me like looking through windows of different coloured glass at many people, times, and places; my task is that of a window-cleaner, making it possible for others both to see through clearly and pass over to find pasture, as I do among such friends. The message of these writers is certainly not one of ease and comfortableness, but of faith, hope, and love. Only after wrestling with God, like Jacob in the dark, and being like him permanently wounded, can anyone go towards the brother one has hated and say, "I see your face as the face of God" (Gen. 33:10). They all used their own life experience, starting where they were, to express the impact on them of the Gospel through self-knowledge and God-knowledge, by submission and repentance, coming closer always to the reality of God in Christ. They spoke out of lives lived within and on behalf of a world as torn and agonizing and filled with doubt as our own.

There are many written sources to draw upon in understanding the inner life of our predecessors in these islands. They were human beings like ourselves, and in exploring their journeys we can be refreshed and encouraged in our own. A search for their backgrounds could begin with the records of the evangelisation of the sixth-century Germanic settlers in Britain who came from different places: there were the existing British Christians, the missionaries sent by Gregory I from Rome, and contacts with Christian Gaul, as well as missionaries and preachers from Ireland and Iona. In effect, the message they brought came originally from Rome, coloured by the different ethos of each group, and they intermingled freely, creating eventually a homogeneous Christian nation out of disparate tribes and peoples.

The chief sources for knowing about them at this early stage are the works of the Venerable Bede (635–736), the greatest scholar of his age and the only Englishman to have been accorded the title of Doctor of the Church. He made it his life's work to offer the new Christians the traditions of Mediterranean Christianity, linking them with the world of the New Testament and the Fathers of the Church, not just as a part of the past, but as life here and now for a new and living people of God.

The basis of Anglo-Saxon spirituality was thus formed by love and not by force. Augustine began by praying and fasting in a small church with the queen and her court, establishing a lasting link between church and state which was dependent on unity of prayer and reality of conduct. This link is seen clearly in the conclusion of the Synod of Whitby where a major division was healed not by reasoned argument or political force but by trust in the resurrection: "King Oswiu said, 'Since Peter is the doorkeeper I will not contradict him, lest when I come to the gates of heaven there may be no-one to open them.'"[1]

In a rough world, existing ways of life were not so much destroyed as transformed: a love of the glory of gold became a love for the beauty of holiness. Awareness of the terrors of both nature and super nature around them, as well as of sin within, led to a strong emphasis on penance, personal as well as corporate, which coloured devotion and affirmed the centrality of the Cross and the Last Judgement. Love of a lord was transferred to love of the high King of Heaven, and love of kin could be the basis of care for members of the Church. This instinctive need for companionship was transferred also to the saints, who were known as always present and always available in prayers, miracles, and visions.

1   Bede, *Ecclesiastical History*, Bk. 3, cap. 25, p. 307.

Bede preserved for us details of this lived Christianity in stories which show the ideals which inspired the new Christians. This was done orally by preaching but also by using the new technology of writing. Augustine had brought with him to a non-literate society a silver cross and an icon of Christ, but also a book which would change the ways of communication forever. He offered these to King Ethelbert and his thanes as tokens of "a new and better kingdom."[2] His approach was in line with the policies of Pope Gregory the Great who sent him, in that he was prepared to build on the existing ideals and customs of the English and transfigure rather than destroy. A serious, practical, and lasting spirituality was the result, based on the Scriptures and the liturgy of the Church, which is illustrated by the cover of this book, which shows the picture of Christ in majesty. It is taken from the *Codex Amiatinus*, the oldest copy of the Latin Vulgate, which was made at Wearmouth Jarrow in Bede's time, thus presenting the Bible as the main window into the light which shone through the lives of our friends.

The sense of living in the ante-chamber of heaven, with the shadow of judgement as well as the promise of mercy always present, coloured all aspects of later medieval devotion, but the eleventh century saw a turning point towards a more personal interior approach. The key figure in this was the theologian-monk Anselm of Bec, who ended his life as archbishop of Canterbury (1033–1109). He made a break with the long tradition of prayer which flowed mainly through the channels of the psalms by creating out of them a new kind of poetic material for the use of anyone who wanted to pray. His *Prayers and Meditations* arose out of his own private prayer, and he sent copies of them to those of his friends who asked for them, together with simple and practical advice about how they could be used. Naturally his prayers were shaped by his monastic background and interests, but from the first they were

2 Ibid., Bk. 1, cap. 25, p. 75.

popular with men and women living a busy Christian life in society for whom the monastic life of prayer was an ideal with which they longed to be associated. Anselm's secretary and biographer, Eadmer, wrote of these prayers:

> With what fear, with what hope and love he addressed himself to God and his saints and taught others to do the same. If the reader will only study them reverently, I hope that his heart will be touched and that he will feel the benefit of them and rejoice in them and for them.[3]

Anselm saw no rift between Christian thought and Christian devotion. As well as being a good pastor, a man of prayer, and an affectionate friend, Anselm was an outstanding scholar, with one of the keenest minds of all time, and he applied his intellect to the lifelong task of thinking about and living for God. Every part of his fine mental equipment was stretched to its limit, seeking and desiring God in practise as well as in thought. At the end of the *Proslogion* he wrote:

> My God,
>
> I pray that I may so know you and love you
>
> that I may rejoice in you
>
> and if I may not do so fully in this life,
>
> let me go steadily on
>
> to the day when I come to that fullness.[4]

It is clear from this quotation, which comes from the last part of his most brilliant philosophical work in which he first proposed what was later called "the ontological argument" for the existence

---

3 Eadmer, *Life of St Anselm*, Bk. 1, cap. viii, p. 14.
4 *Prayers and Meditations of St Anselm*, ll. 791–800.

of God, that Anselm knew very well that God is not known by the intellect on its own but by the heart and mind together. His own discovery about prayer was what he passed on to others as "faith seeking understanding." In his advice about praying, he insisted that the first necessity was to want to pray and be ready to give up some part at least of concern with oneself in order to be "free a while for God." In a quiet place, alone, Anselm offered the person praying words that he himself had prayed, arising out of, but not confined to, the Scriptures used in personal and intimate dialogue with Jesus.

It is possible to find the same approach in Julian of Norwich (1342–1413.) Julian composed two books, one a long version of the other, called *Revelations of Divine Love*, expressing the flowering of English prose as well as containing the first sustained theology to be written in English. She lived as an anchoress in a cell built onto the wall of the church of St. Julian in Norwich. In the twentieth century, she became well known and indeed popular, but she was very little known in her own times and all but lost sight of at the Reformation. Her works were recovered and edited only at the end of the nineteenth century, as if they had been preserved especially for our times. Her theology was based on a background of immense global suffering and despair. The time and opportunity for a peaceful life was challenged in the most basic manner possible by universal attacks of a fatal plague, called the Black Death, which struck at everyone and recurred; it was almost impossible to assuage.

There are so many deeds which in our eyes are evilly done and lead to such great harms that it seems impossible to us that any good result should ever come from them.[5]

5 Julian of Norwich, *Revelations*, cap. 87.

She was well aware of the sinful state of all: "I saw and understood that we may not in this life keep us from sin as completely as we shall in heaven." But she was sure that here and now we should not despair: "Neither on the one hand should we fall low in despair, nor on the other be over reckless as if we did not care but we should simply acknowledge that we may not stand for the twinkling of an eye except by the grace of God and we should reverently cleave to God in him only trusting."[6]

With this dark background of fatal illness and continuous warfare the poet Langland (1332–1400) presented a vision of realistic but loving hope similar to that encountered in Julian:

> I dreamt a marvellous dream;
> I was in a wilderness I could not tell where . . .
> and between the tower and the gulf
> I saw a smooth field full of folk,
> high and low together. (*Piers Plowman*)

The tower of truth and the gulf of sorrow: and between them a field full of folk. This vision is concerned with the folk between these two extremes, and in some ways, it is a true vision of Christian life in any time or place. There is always a dynamic unity between the content of a faith (the "tower of truth") and the way it is lived out ("the gulf of sorrow") not by a special elite but by the "folk" themselves. Spirituality cannot be seen as a pure intellectual stream of consciousness flowing from age to age among articulate people only; it is always the lens of the gospel placed over each age, each place, each person.

This unity of understanding within the changing settings of the disasters and challenges of life can be seen in Bede, Cuthbert, and Anselm. Alongside them are the hermits of the twelfth century, and

6 Ibid.

the fourteenth-century writers Julian of Norwich and Langland. Andrewes, Taylor, and Frank in the seventeenth century show how the same approach to inner pilgrimage continued in changing social contexts, a stream of ever-moving pilgrims going towards the life of heaven.

We are all engaged in this pilgrimage with them, and there is refreshment in such companionship. We are all Bunyan's Christian, and as well as being his Mr. Despair, we are also his Faithful-unto-Death. We with him will cross over in the loving company of friends, where for us as for him "all the trumpets sounded for him on the other side." Between the tower of truth and the gulf of sorrow our predecessors stood, as we do, within a field full of folk with only one rule: "Give love and receive the kingdom!"

BENEDICTA WARD, Oxford, 2018

1

THE SPIRITUALITY
of ST. CUTHBERT

◆ ■ ◆ ■ ◆ ■ ◆ ■ ◆ ■ ◆ ■ ◆ ■ ◆

I n his preface to *Two Lives of St Cuthbert*, Bertram Colgrave
wrote, "These Lives of St Cuthbert throw considerable light on
the secular history of the golden age of Northumbria. They also
illustrate one of the most important periods in the history of the
English Church."[7] Rarely has an historian been so prophetic. Since
then, scholarship has continued to illustrate the truth of that comment,
showing each year how the *Lives of St Cuthbert*, combined with the
study of art, archaeology, and artefacts, as well as charters and laws,
does indeed throw light upon many facets of life in Northumbria in
the seventh century. Moreover, it has been equally clear that the cult
of St. Cuthbert, like so many saints' lives, throws even more light upon
many and varied facets of later medieval life, whether in the times of
the Danish invasions, the monastic revival, or the Norman Conquest.
There is much profit in exploring the *Lives* in this way; but how it would
have surprised Bede, let alone Cuthbert. For Bede did not write his *Life
of St Cuthbert* to provide later historians with interesting information
about "the secular history of the golden age of Northumbria," nor was
he intending to give later readers a biography in the style of Boswell,
of Cuthbert in His Times. It is right to look carefully at the form of the
work and examine its sources and antecedents, to see it as a reflection
of its cultural setting, to look at the audience for which such a work

7 *Two Lives of St Cuthbert*, ed. and trans. Bertram Colgrave (New York: Cambridge
University Press, 1985), vii.

was intended, but it seems only fair to try also to see what Bede himself wanted to convey in his picture of Cuthbert.

The "horizontal" approach to Cuthbert as a man related to other men needs to be complemented by the "vertical" approach to Cuthbert as he related to God, for in the *Life of St Cuthbert*, both in verse and in prose, Bede, like the anonymous writer before him, was writing the life of a saint; the form of their texts and the content of them were both part of the tradition of Christian hagiography. Their aim was to show that Cuthbert was holy—that is, that he showed in his life the marks of Christ crucified and that God had shown his love for that life of discipleship by signs and wonders, before and after death, just as he had done in the case of other holy ones in earlier times and other places. Moreover, their aim was to write in such a way that Cuthbert's holiness should continue to have meaning in the lives of others. A hagiography is above all pragmatic, practical: it shows one of that great cloud of witnesses in the detail of his life on earth as he walked in the footsteps of the Man of Galilee; and it poses the invitation of the angels at the tomb: "Come and see; he is not here, he is risen." The accounts of Cuthbert are not only a window onto the dead past; they are a stream of living water where he who is alive in Christ shows the race that is set before those who come after. They are not rather poor biographies; they are first-rate hagiographies.

I intend, therefore, to speak about the spirituality of Cuthbert, as about something alive and immediate. But at once there are problems in even getting beyond the first word. What is spirituality? It is not a word Cuthbert would have recognized or, indeed, a medieval word at all. Its earlier use in the plural, *spiritualities*, referred to spiritual jurisdiction as opposed to temporal jurisdiction, the "lords spiritual" as opposed (and how often literally opposed) to the "lords temporal." *Spiritualité* has, of course, undergone a later transformation, and in its French form there is a very good chance that *un spirituel* will be someone who is witty, lively, or even mad. These are not the uses of the word Dr. Stancliffe had in mind when she asked me to talk about the spirituality of St. Cuthbert. There is another use of the word *spirituality* nowadays, which I regard with caution, since it seems vaguely gnostic, in which it means the non-material aspect of things, as in the "spirituality of the motor bike," the "spirituality of progress," the "spirituality of electronics": a passive use of the phrase, referring, I hope, to human reaction to these objects. A more active use of the phrase is current in the "spirituality of Islamic culture," and this is closer to the use I want to make of the term. To see the desires and religious aspirations of men within their cultural context can be extremely illuminating, especially in connection with non-literate societies. But as far as Cuthbert is concerned, it has its limits, partly because much of the information about his society comes in fact from the *Life* itself; but also because this is still an approach which differs from that of the writers of the earliest *Lives*. I prefer, therefore, to take a middle way, and combine this modern use of the word *spirituality* (which is perhaps closer to "mentality") with another meaning given to it in the nineteenth century when it was coined. It was used then to describe a field of study earlier called ascetic theology, and/or mystical prayer. By "spirituality," then, I mean what Cuthbert himself thought and said and did and prayed in the light of the Gospel of Christ. It seems to me that both Bede and Cuthbert would recognize this approach.

But this at once poses another problem, for what can be known about this inner kingdom? The way to know the heart of a man of the past is usually through his writings, and nothing survives directly from Cuthbert himself. He is seen only through the lens of observers, and moreover, neither of his earliest biographers ever met him. That is

surely a perilous way to see anyone, especially when I am proposing to
look at what Thomas Merton described as

> a point of pure truth, [at the centre of our being] a point or
> spark which belongs entirely to God, which is never at our
> disposal, from which God disposes of our lives, which is in-
> accessible to the fantasies of our mind or the brutalities of our
> own will.[8]

It is rare to reach any awareness of that kind of spirituality in
oneself—how much less in others; but it is such a centre that illuminates
and governs thought, word, and action, and by looking wisely at the
external moments, some apprehension of the centre can be touched. I
want to suggest that the early *Lives of St Cuthbert* give us that wise view;
but before examining them to come near the inner life of Cuthbert as
he faced towards Christ, there is one obvious method of narrowing the
scope of the inquiry. That is by saying at once what his life of prayer
was not: it was not, for instance, the rosary, it was not the Stations of
the Cross, it was not matins and evensong, and it was not the piety of
fourth-century Egypt, or eleventh-century Canterbury, or sixteenth-
century Spain. Cuthbert was not a monk of Jarrow in the days of Bede,
nor was he a monk of Durham, either in the time of Symeon or in the
time of Reginald; nor was he Benedictine in any sense whatever; and
he was not a Sister of the Love of God, either.

That is rather a negative comment; but perhaps it has at least been
a warning signal not to shape Cuthbert in our own image. He was
a man of his own time and place, and much about him ought to be
alien, strange, perhaps at times entirely opaque. But while bearing that
essential element of otherness in mind, I want to suggest that there
is a more positive approach possible to Cuthbert. After all, there is a

---

8 Thomas Merton, *Conjectures of a Guilty Bystander* (New York: Image Books,
1968), 142.

minimum of fact about Cuthbert which is agreed upon even by the severest historians: he actually lived. No one has ever suggested—as they have with both St. Antony of Egypt and St. Benedict of Nursia— that he was made up. And he lived in Northumbria in the mid-seventh century. He chose to be a monk and hermit, and he was also a bishop. I suggest that it can safely be inferred also that Cuthbert, noble or poor, was a man for whom his Christian life was a serious matter, and that his friends and colleagues were also men of integrity and not hypocrites. Cuthbert was known to them as a man of prayer, like them concerned primarily with what Jeremy Taylor called "following after the most holy Jesus, which is truest religion and most solemn adoration."[9] It was two such men, Cuthbert's near contemporaries, following a way of life very like his own, who wrote about him fairly soon after his death, while there were still people alive who had known him well. They also were neither fools nor liars but men of excellent intelligence and literary competence, one of them the first in the great tradition of English historians. The question these men asked about Cuthbert may not be ours, but it is a valid one; they were not interested in his noble connections, his love of gold, beer, or small animals, not even whether he was clever, brave, or great; they only wanted to know how this frail human being had put on the Lord Jesus Christ through life and into death. There are always those who do and those who write, and the life of Cuthbert was made articulate by those who wrote about him. They chose small pictures from his life and presented them with a wealth of interpretation directed to elucidating this central theme.

With this agreed minimum of fact in mind, and accepting the innate honesty of the writers in terms of their own concerns, I suggest that there is one way in which these, and indeed other, hagiographies

9 Jeremy Taylor, *The Life of Our Blessed Lord and Saviour, Jesus Christ, the Great Exemplar of Sanctity and Holy Life*, in *Complete Works*, ed. R. Heber, revised J. Eden, 6 vols. (London, 1847), vol. II, 47–48.

can shed light upon their subject. In 1987, in the cathedral church of Durham, the manuscript of the Lindisfarne Gospels was placed on the grave of Cuthbert; I suggest that this is what both the anonymous monk of Lindisfarne and Bede did in their *Lives* of St. Cuthbert: they placed over Cuthbert's life the Bible. With that overwhelmingly beautiful book, the Lindisfarne Gospels, the most beautiful thing about it is not its decoration but its content, the Gospel, the Good News, of Jesus Christ; just so the most important parts of the *Lives* of St. Cuthbert are not in the beauty of detail, but in those things that link Cuthbert with the biblical tradition of sanctity, which is done most of all by the quotations the writers give from the Scriptures. In a first glance through a hagiography or any ancient text, the modern eye tends to skip the biblical quotations as mere pious trimming. I believe this to be an error of method. The illuminations of the Lindisfarne Gospels take on a world of new meaning if seen in connection with the text; the inner meaning of the *Lives* of St. Cuthbert is made clearer, not more obscure, by examining the parts of the Scriptures that are placed over that life.

The best text for this examination is the prose *Life* by Bede, preeminently a man of the Bible, whom Boniface called "that keen investigator of the Holy Scriptures";[10] and for Bede, the text of the Bible was not read alone. The Fathers of the Church had read the sacred page and commented on its various layers of meaning, in the conviction that the Holy Spirit was continually revealing the full truth of the written word, and it is just these interpretations that Bede collected and extended in his commentaries on the Bible. It seems to me useful, therefore, to examine the biblical quotations used by Bede, and to some extent by the anonymous writer, in connection with the standard

---

10 *Letters of St. Boniface,* trans. Ephraim Emerton (New York: Columbia University Press, 2000), Letter to Ecgberht, no. 75, p. 168 (= ep. no. 91 in Tangl edition).

patristic interpretations of those passages, which were familiar to those reading the *Lives* as they no longer are to most of us. Such study is particularly illuminating in this case since very often Bede himself gave the common interpretations of the texts in his commentaries on the Scriptures. The texts can be used as a lens held over the life of Cuthbert to show more distinctly the intimacies of a life lived in the light of the sacred page. It is possible that what will emerge most of all will be the spirituality of Bede, but I think this is not altogether the case.

Bede looked deeply into the *Life* already written at Lindisfarne, and in his metrical *Life* he had already pointed out the interior meaning of many episodes, using the *Life* as he used the Scriptures.[11] With the information about Cuthbert before him, supplemented by other sources, he set about presenting the inner significance of the text. This was the common approach to a text in the ancient world, where the surface meaning was seen as a thin layer, beyond which lay riches for the taking, and this was pre-eminently true of the text of the Bible as both Bede and Cuthbert used it. Such meditation of the text was to them common ground, not a different way of looking at things. While Cuthbert had never seen the Lindisfarne Gospels, he knew the Scriptures so well that he staked his life on the message they contain.

In writing his account of Cuthbert, Bede is using the Scriptures as a lens, but it need not be a distorting lens. It is necessary to be alert in case what is revealed is the spirituality of the observers, for one sees what one is able to see, what one expects to be there; and, indeed, there is no objective observer of saints. Some of what the anonymous monk and Bede wrote is coloured by their own prejudices, and more is coloured by a standard tradition of hagiography. Yet the early *Lives* are the nearest documents to Cuthbert in time; they come from men with

11 Cf. Michael Lapidge, "The Metrical Life of St. Cuthbert," in *St. Cuthbert, His Cult and His Community to A.D. 1200,* ed. Gerald Bonner et al. (Rochester, NY: Boydell & Brewer, 1989), 86–93.

similar preoccupations, they are directly concerned with Cuthbert's spirituality, and they are especially sensitive to the words of the Scriptures which formed the basis of his life. It seems to me, therefore, at least instructive not to try to sift factual detail from hagiographical *topos* in the *Lives* but rather to examine certain biblical texts that Bede and, to some extent, the anonymous writer also used to convey their understanding of the inner life of Cuthbert. Since it would be a very lengthy task to look at all the quotations from the Bible in the *Lives*, I want to look at the use of three biblical quotations which are used at key points in the *Life of St Cuthbert* and see what they convey about the inner truth of the stories they illustrate.

The first text I want to examine is the account, which only Bede gives, of the monastic education of Cuthbert at Melrose, which he says he heard from Herefrith of Lindisfarne, who knew it from Cuthbert himself. Cuthbert was received at Melrose by Boisil, and after his sojourn at Ripon returned there, where "most diligently he paid heed both to the words and the deeds of the blessed Boisil as he had been accustomed to do before."[12] Boisil died of a plague which had affected Cuthbert also. Herefrith, a priest of Lindisfarne and later abbot there, who was in the monastery at the time, told Bede how, in the last week of his life, Boisil proposed to spend his time teaching his disciple:

> Cuthbert . . . answered, "And what, I ask you, is it best for me to read, which I can yet finish in one week?" He replied, "The evangelist John. I have a book consisting of seven gatherings of which we can get through one every day, with the Lord's help, reading it and discussing it between ourselves so far as is necessary."[13]

12 *Vita sancti Cuthberti auctore anonymo,* Bede's prose *Life of St Cuthbert,* ed. and trans. Bertram Colgrave in *Two Lives of St Cuthbert,* op. cit., 180–81 (henceforth abbreviated to *VCP,* and cited by book).
13 Ibid., 182–83.

Fifty years later, perhaps these words were remembered at another death-bed and with another Cuthbert: "There is still one sentence not completed, dear master." "Then write it quickly." "Now it is done."[14] Bede's last anxious gift to the Anglo-Saxon Christians was a translation of St. John; perhaps it was the story told him by Herefrith that so moved Bede that he chose to communicate St. John to others at his own death. There are three points I want to make about this passage. First, why did two teachers offer St. John to their Anglo-Saxon converts? How did they understand him? St. John's is called "the eagle Gospel" by St. Jerome, in his preface which was as well known as the text, because it is "about the divinity of Christ . . . the rest of contemplation . . . the mysteries of God."[15] It is this fact of the divinity of Christ that Boisil conveys to his disciple in those last days as the fundamental basis of faith.

Secondly, not only the content, but fact that they spent seven days in reading, was significant for Bede. Bede devotes some time in his commentary on Genesis to the mystical meaning of six and eight, relating such measurements of time to the whole work of creation and re-creation, in which the eighth day is the everlasting day of the great Easter of heaven.[16] So it was not lightly said that they read the Gospel together for seven days, for the eighth was the entry of Boisil into heaven, into the rest of the day that is forever.

Thirdly, and for Bede this was the most important aspect of the story, he saw significance in the way in which they read the Scriptures: "They dealt with the simple things of 'the faith that works by

---

14 *Venerabilis Baedae Opera historica,* ed. C. Plummer, 2 vols. (Oxford, 1896), I, pp. clxii–clxiv, *De Obitu Baedae.*

15 Jerome, "Preface to the Gospels", *Biblia Sacra juxta Vulgatem Versionem,* ed. B. Fisher et al., 2 vols. (Stuttgart, 1983), II, p. 1516.

16 Bede, *Libri Quattuor in principium Genesis usque ad nativitatem Isaac et eiectionam Ismahelis adnotationum,* ed. C. W. Jones, Corpus Christianorum, Series Latina 118A (Turnhout, 1953—), p. 103.

love' (Gal. 5: 6)."[17] A later commentary expressed exactly Bede's understanding of this verse from Galatians as being about faith which finds its expression in love:

> Without love faith is useless; faith with love is Christian. Otherwise it is demonic. The devils also believe and tremble (James 2:19). Those who do not believe are lower and worse than the demons. But there is a great difference whether one believes Him to be Christ or believes in Christ. Even the devils believe Him to be Christ; he who believes in Christ, however, is he who hopes in Christ and loves him.[18]

In these seven days of reading, Boisil "declared all Cuthbert's future to him,"[19] but this was no special and secret revelation or prophecy; Boisil's insight into Cuthbert's future came *because* they were reading the Scriptures, not apart from it. This reading became in itself the fundamental basis for the whole of Cuthbert's life as a servant of God. This light from the sacred page was to lead Cuthbert to Farne; but even more, as Boisil saw, it was to bring him back to the service of "the faith that works by love" as bishop.

On the island, Cuthbert was alone, sealed into prayer, grounded more and more into faith; as monk, and especially as bishop, he did not stay in a cell or even in a monastery. He was always away, preaching, weeping with the penitent, in the faith that finds its issue in love. The biblical context of the quotation underlines the training Boisil gave through St. John's Gospel: "for in Christ Jesus there is neither circumcision nor uncircumcision but the faith that works by love" (Gal. 5:6).

---

17 *VCP* 8, p. 182.
18 Walafrid Strabo, *Glossa Ordinaria*, "Epistola ad Galatas," PL 114, cols. 582–83.
19 *VCP* 8, p. 182.

As bishop, Cuthbert was not a monk's monk, nor did he confine himself to a select group; his teaching was for the poor and needy, and his companions were lay men and even women. The close walk with God that he knew on Farne came from the light of the Scriptures as he read them with Boisil, and that love of God issued in the service of love for all. He was not a divided man torn by two vocations, the one to solitude, the other to service, but someone who from the basis of faith did the works of love whatever the circumstances. In his *Ecclesiastical History of the English Nation,* Bede's final summary of Cuthbert's life is that he "received from [Boisil] knowledge of the Scriptures and the example of a life of good works."[20] *Verbo et exemplo docere*: his was a faith exercised both in solitude and in preaching to the poor.

My second example is perhaps the most familiar section of the *Life of St Cuthbert.* Cuthbert, as a monk of Melrose, was invited to visit Aebbe, the abbess of Coldingham, and sister of King Oswiu. Coldingham was a monastery which, it seems from Bede's *Ecclesiastical History,* may have needed all the instruction, both in word and example, that its royal abbess could get for it. When the Irish ascetic Adomnan saw the abbey some years later, he wept and told the abbess that the behaviour of her community was a scandal:

All of them, men and women alike, are sunk in slothful slumber or else they remain awake for the purposes of sin. And the cells that were built for praying and for reading have become haunts of feasting, drinking, gossip, and other delights; even the virgins who are dedicated to God put aside all respect for their profession and, whenever they have leisure, spend their time

20 *Bede's Ecclesiastical History of the English People,* ed. and trans. B. Colgrave and R. A. B. Mynors (Oxford: Oxford Medieval Texts, 1969), pp. 432–33.

weaving elaborate garments with which to adorn themselves as
if they were brides, so imperilling their virginity, or else to make
friends with strange men.[21]

The frivolity of the young nuns of Coldingham raises a smile now,
but no one smiled at the time; to assume the life of a monk or nun
was a serious matter, even for royalty. Decadence was not accepted as
either normal or nice. Such a relaxed state of affairs was dangerous,
and it could hardly be the work of a few years. When Cuthbert visited
it was, perhaps, this atmosphere of scarcely subdued eroticism which
troubled him. For when he prayed at night, as was his custom, he went
to the beach to stand in the icy waters of the sea, that old monastic
remedy for lust.

What happened when he returned to the sand illustrates another
theme altogether:

> There followed in his footsteps two little sea-animals, humbly
> prostrating themselves on the earth; and, licking his feet, they
> rolled upon them, wiping them with their skins and warming
> them with their breath.[22]

A walk on the beach at night, so often fruitful for the English! A man
alone by the sea, singing to himself and taking a dip, with small furry
animals rubbing round his ankles. How attractive; is this, perhaps—
and how consoling it would be—the spirituality of Cuthbert? But this
most private, intimate moment of the prayer of Cuthbert is not so
superficial for either the anonymous writer or Bede when they place
over it the lens of the Scriptures. For the anonymous writer Cuthbert is
Daniel, thrown into danger of lust, as Daniel was thrown into the den

21 Ibid., pp. 424–27.
22 *Vita sancti Cuthberti auctore anonymo*, the anonymous *Life of St Cuthbert*, ed.
    and trans. B. Colgrave, in *Two Lives*, op. cit., pp. 80–81 (henceforth abbreviated
    to *VCA*, and cited by book and chapter); cf. *VCP* 10.

of lions; and Cuthbert, like Daniel, is ministered to by the animals.[23] For the Fathers of the Church, Daniel was never just the eunuch of King Nebuchadnezzar. He was Christ, who "thought it not robbery to be equal with God but emptied himself" (Phil. 2: 7), and came down, a new Daniel, into this animal den of the world. For Bede the emphasis is different though equally scriptural; he uses the words of the Gospel spoken by Jesus to his disciples after the Transfiguration: "Tell the vision to no man until the Son of Man be risen again from the dead" (Matt. 17: 9).

In his commentary on the Transfiguration,[24] Bede restated the patristic understanding of this moment of vision as the second epiphany of Christ, parallel to the Baptism of Christ in the Jordan, the two revelations of the Christ as the Son of God. The "vision" seen on the shore of the North Sea centuries later was, for Bede, the same epiphany of God, by water and by light. It was a moment of such awe and terror that the observer, like the disciples, "was stricken with . . . deadly fear."[25] He had not been watching a man on a beach with his pets; he had seen the face of Christ in a man so transfigured in prayer that the right order of creation was in him restored. For Bede, Cuthbert with the animals was an even more awesome sight than for the anonymous writer: he was the new Adam, once more at peace with all creation, naming the animals, who were the first servants and the first friends. And as in the story of Cuthbert and Boisil, this is also a scene which leads towards entry into the kingdom through the gateway that is called death.

There are two other points Bede is making here: one is that Cuthbert, renewed and purged by prayer, goes to "[sing] the canonical hymns with the brethren":[26] the common life of charity and praise,

23 VCA II, 3, pp. 82–83.
24 Bede, *In Lucae evangelium expositio*, ed. D. Hurst, Corpus Christianorum Series Latina (Turnhout, 1953-), p. 205.
25 VCP 10, pp. 190–91.
26 Ibid., pp. 188–89.

however lax, is still the place for the exercise of the faith that works by love. Secondly, there is a third otter. Bede describes the two otters as "prostrate before him on the sand";[27] and when he describes the cleric of Coldingham, lying trembling before the feet of Cuthbert, he describes him in the same attitude: "he approached Cuthbert and, stretching himself on the ground, tearfully entreated his pardon."[28] The relationship of man with the animals is transfigured easily and naturally in the love and worship of the first two otters, and while the third otter is also taken into that same transfiguration, it is by tears of repentance and through the gate and grave of death.

For my third passage I have chosen the moment when that death was fulfilled; again Bede's source was Herefrith. When the anonymous author describes the death of Cuthbert, he presents a picture of peace and order:

> Being attracted by the love of his former solitary life, he returned to the island. . . . He remained alone, satisfied with the converse and ministry of angels, full of hope and putting his trust wholly in God.[29]

It is a bland description enough, but there is a discreet hint of something harsher in his choice of a phrase from Mark 1:13, where angels ministered to Christ, but after the forty days of temptation in the wilderness. Bede dares to go closer to the last days of Cuthbert through what he heard from Herefrith who was with him, and he makes of it a revelation of the ultimate truth of the life of the saint. Herefrith had described how Cuthbert was left alone on Farne before his death,

27   Ibid., pp. 190–91.
28   Ibid., pp. 188–89.
29   *VCA* IV, 11, pp. 128–29.

suffering in the darkness of a storm for five days.[30] Bad weather had prevented Herefrith's return to the sick man, and Cuthbert had been also subject to a tempest both external and interior. He had dragged himself to the hut on the shore, out of a great courtesy towards the brothers who would come back, and Herefrith found him there, without food or drink, his face marked by disease and pain. It was not a quiet and interesting illness that he was suffering but a disgusting sore that suppurated. And he had endured also that ultimate terror, about which Herefrith says he did not dare to inquire. It was surely the dereliction which is at the heart of the Gospel, when God was forsaken by God.

This last darkness of the saints in their union with Christ is the most fundamental part of Christian sanctity, and perhaps the most difficult to approach. It is not, I think, something interesting to endure nor a particularly spiritual condition. Often it consists in disgusting disease, long pain, loneliness, sometimes the anguish of doubt and despair, helplessness mental as well as physical. And it is not confined to those officially called saints. Perhaps it is not inappropriate to draw a parallel with the last years of a very great medieval historian, Helen Waddell:

> Helen Waddell's life seemingly ceased in the 1950s, with the total eclipse of her dazzling gifts of intellect, winning charm, balance and humour, her ripe scholarship and deep spirituality. Mute, unheeding, unfeeling, blind to all beauty, a stranger to the family she had so loved, she sat day after day before a picture of Christ crucified.[31]

For Helen, the darkness lasted for fifteen years, for Cuthbert, for five days; but time, I think, is not here measured by the clock. It had never been the beauty of the scenery that had drawn Cuthbert to

---

30 VCP 37.
31 Felicitas Corrigan, *Helen Waddell: A Biography* (London, 1986), pp. 355–56.

Farne—indeed he seems to have taken great pains not to see it at all. For him it was the desert, the place of the cross. There was nothing there for Cuthbert but the stars and water among the rocks; and no one had really understood. Whenever the brothers came they got it wrong, right up to their demands for his body after his death. Even Herefrith could not speak clearly about the real significance of the island, and the anonymous writer made no attempt. It was Bede, with his intuitive sympathy for the hermit and the ascetic, who perceived the truth; and it was Bede who provided a clear lens to see both those last mysterious days and the whole meaning of Cuthbert's life on the island. He does so not at the end but at the very beginning of the *Life of St Cuthbert*:

> The prophet Jeremiah consecrates for us the beginning of our account of the life and miracles of the blessed father, Cuthbert, when, praising the hermit's state of perfection, he says: "It is good for a man to have borne the yoke in his youth; he sitteth alone and keepeth silence because he hath borne it upon him."[32]

This is no random phrase from the Old Testament, nor a pious cliché about solitude. The commentary, which gives this passage from Lamentations its solemnity, is from the liturgy rather than the patristic texts, and it is from the readings at night office for the last days of Holy Week in the Office of Tenebrae. The reading of Lamentations at Tenebrae belongs to one of the oldest layers of Christian liturgy,[33] and it seems certain that Bede knew the lessons in this form. When John the Chanter revised the liturgy at Wearmouth/Jarrow,[34] it is more than possible that he introduced there the readings for the last days of Holy

---

32 *VCP* 1, p. 154, and using the Authorized Version of Lam. 3: 28, quoted here.
33 *Dictionaire d'archéologie chrétienne et de liturgie (DACL)*, ed. F. Cabrol and H. Leclercq, 15 vols., (Paris, 1903–53), XV, i, under "Semaine sainte," cols. 1165–69.
34 *Venerabilis Baedae Opera historica*, ed. Plummer, I, 369; Bede, *Lives of the Abbots* 6, trans. D. H. Farmer, in *The Age of Bede*, ed. Farmer (London, 1965/85), p. 190.

Week that were already common in Rome.[35] These included the reading of the Lamentations of Jeremiah at Tenebrae, where they are set among responses about the passion and death of Christ. In one of the most beautiful pieces of liturgy ever written, these verses from Lamentations become the cry of the Crucified: "He sitteth alone and keepeth silence because he hath borne it upon him," with the respond, "He was led as a lamb to the slaughter, and while he was evil entreated he opened not his mouth; he was delivered unto death that he might give life unto his people."[36] It may well have been with this interpretation in mind that Bede used this phrase of Cuthbert, seeing him in his life, and especially in that mysterious darkness before his death, identified with Christ on the Cross through the faith that worked continually by love.

Surely this is the real point about the early *Lives* of Cuthbert. Some actual, physical details about his earthly life are there, but the writers are not directly concerned with them. There is no "spirituality" there, if by that is meant the personal mental activities of Cuthbert when he prayed or when he taught. What the *Lives* do contain is a series of pictures of real events presented for their significance in relation to God. There is no way of stripping these stories of their piety in the hopes of finding a familiar and accessible figure at the centre. The anonymous writer and Bede do not write in that way. They use passages of the Scriptures that Cuthbert himself knew, and by which he lived, to illuminate the whole man. What they show, like all Christian hagiography, is that the words and deeds of this human being were gradually entirely filled, transfigured, with the presence of God in Christ reconciling the world to himself. A Christian saint is not remembered as wise or great or righteous, but as a humble and sinful human being who learned, through who knows what agonies and darknesses, so to walk in faith

35 Cf. Cabrol and Leclercq, *DACL* XV, i, col. 1166, and XII, ii, cols. 2436–37 (under "*Ordines romani*").
36 Office of Tenebrae, Holy Saturday, First Nocturn.

in Christ through his daily life that at the point of death he revealed to others, if not to himself, that underneath are the everlasting arms.

The hagiographer is one who shows this life of discipleship to readers for their encouragement and imitation. In the three passages examined from the *Life of St Cuthbert*, I do not at all suggest that the events did not take place, but that in each case the meaning of them is revealed by the use of Scripture. At Melrose it is not Cuthbert's education linked to miraculous prophecy that is presented, but the whole basis of his life is shown to have been set by an acceptance of the faith that does the works of love. By the North Sea at Coldingham, Cuthbert was no animal lover out for a walk, but the new Adam in whom the right ordering of creation was restored. And on Farne, the writers do not give a picture of a busy bishop longing to get away from it all to a lovely island with nature and scenery: they bring the reader into the presence of a man crucified with Christ, alone and keeping silence as he accepts death.

Such was the force of this love in this human being that after death his flesh continued to shine with wholeness and his living presence on the other side of Christ continued to be a refuge, the shadow of a mighty rock within a weary land. At the place where his body lay, in the sure and certain hope of a glorious resurrection, the poor and needy and terrified continued to find peace. It seemed ominously appropriate to Bede that when Cuthbert died the monks of Lindisfarne were singing Psalm 60, "O God thou hast cast us out and scattered us abroad," and he tells the reader to note how the whole of that psalm was fulfilled afterwards.[37] But when he ended his prose *Life of St Cuthbert,* he used a different psalm, Psalm 103, a psalm not of judgement but of mercy and blessing. That is surely the

37   *VCP* 40, pp. 286–87.

final message of Cuthbert, who did not leave his humble successor on Farne, Felgild, to endure deformity and pain, but cured him so that

> his face had always been free from this affliction, through the grace of Almighty God, who in this present age is wont to heal many, and, in time to come, will heal our diseases of mind and body; for he satisfies our desire with good things and crowns us for ever with "loving kindness and tender mercies."[38]

APPENDIX

Some Dates for St. Cuthbert

596   Coming of Augustine to Kent; baptism of Aethelberht of Kent.

627   Baptism of Edwin of Northumbria.

632   Death of Edwin.

c. 634   Birth of Cuthbert.

c. 635   Oswald of Northumbria assisted by Aidan of Iona; foundation of monastery of Lindisfarne.

      Death of Oswald at battle of Maserfield; Northumbria divided between Oswini in Deira and Oswiu in Bernicia.

642   Cuthbert given into care of his foster-mother, Kenswith. Military service for Cuthbert.

651   Oswine murdered by order of Oswiu. Death of Aidan.

      Cuthbert enters Melrose Abbey aged 17, taught by Boisil.

655   Battle of the Winwaed and supremacy of Oswiu in Northumbria.

c. 657   Cuthbert goes to a new monastery at Ripon with Eata and acts as guest-master until they return to Melrose, c. 660.

      Cuthbert survives the plague of which Boisil died, c. 664.

664   Council of Whitby.

      Cuthbert Prior of Melrose. Visit to Aebbe of Coldingham.

---

38 *VCP* 46, pp. 305–7.

673 Bede born.

c. 666 Cuthbert to Lindisfarne. Eata Abbot of Lindisfarne, Cuthbert Prior of Lindisfarne.

Cuthbert to Farne as a hermit.

680 Death of Hilda of Whitby. Council of Hatfield. Bede entered Wearmouth, aged seven.

685 Cuthbert consecrated bishop and exchanges his See of Hexham for See of Lindisfarne.

686 Return of Cuthbert to Farne.

687 Death of Cuthbert on Farne. Burial at Lindisfarne.

689 Translation of St. Cuthbert's incorrupt body.

699 Composition of the *Anonymous Life* at Lindisfarne.

c. 705 Bede writes his metrical *Life of St Cuthbert*.

c. 721 Bede's *Prose Life of St Cuthbert* written at request of Eadfrith of Lindisfarne.

731 Completion of Bede's *Ecclesiastical History* containing his summary of the life of St. Cuthbert (Bk. iv, caps. xxvii-xxii).

1104 Cuthbert translated to tomb in new cathedral in Durham.

2
BEDE AND THE CONVERSION
of the ANGLO-SAXONS

❖ ■ ❖ ■ ❖ ■ ❖ ■ ❖ ■ ❖ ■ ❖ ■ ❖

The *Ecclesiastical History of the English People* was completed by the Venerable Bede in "the year of our Lord 731," a chronological calculation for which he himself was responsible, and which was to have a more lasting influence on European thought than even his histories and biblical commentaries. Living as a simple monk in a monastery in the north of that *alter orbis*, Britain, which seemed to the men of the Mediterranean world the very edge of civilization, in a land with no tradition of learning, whose people had been converted to Christianity only fifty years before, Bede nevertheless became the most learned man of his age and the first, and perhaps still the greatest, of the historians of England. His reputation among his contemporaries was as a commentator of the Scriptures. Boniface, writing to England with requests for books to help in the conversion of Germany half a century later, asked for the works of "that keen investigator of the Scriptures, the monk Bede"[39]; ". . . a spark," he called him, "from the light of the Church which the Holy spirit has kindled in your land."[40] And Bede himself says of his own life, "I have spent all my life in this monastery, applying myself entirely to the study of the Holy Scriptures."[41] His fame later was, and is, as the inventor and popularizer of the dating of our

39 *Letters of Saint Boniface*, trans. Ephraim Emerton, *Records of Civilization: Sources and Studies* XXXI (New York: Columbia University Press, 1940), Letter LXI (70), 134.
40 Ibid., Letter LIX (75), 133.
41 Bede's *Ecclesiastical History of the English People*, ed. and trans. B. Colgrave and R. A. B. Mynors (Oxford, 1972), 566. This source is hereafter referred to as *EHEP*.

era by the year of grace AD, from the Incarnation of Christ, thus giving a framework to our consideration of past and present which underlies all our thought.

But it is Bede's historical work, the *Ecclesiastical History of the English People*, which is today the most popular of his works and the most widely read. The work of a very great historian, whose critical standards would be admirable in any historian of today, it provides the main source for the early history of England, and is unique in its scope and accuracy as well as in its readability. It is a great and rich work, within which I will draw attention to two aspects only: first, the interaction of religion and politics in the world Bede describes, and secondly, the extent to which paganism remained close to the surface in this newly baptized people.

The conversion of the Anglo-Saxon invaders of Britain to Christianity as seen by Bede a generation later is a remarkable story, full of life and vigour. In it, the interweaving of religion and politics is so close that it is impossible to treat them separately, a fact to bear in mind, incidentally, when considering the history of the Church in England later. There were two main areas of missionary activity to begin with: the Italians in Kent and the Irish in Northumbria. In both cases, the preaching of the missionaries, indeed their very presence in the island, was dependent on the good will of the kings. Even where, as in Kent, the missionaries had the friendship of the queen, already a Christian, the good will of the king was vital before they could stay and live in his territory at all. In 596, Augustine landed in Kent and was given by the king, Ethelbert, "a dwelling in the city of Canterbury, the chief city of all his dominions"[42] with freedom to worship and to preach. But Ethelbert himself did not receive baptism until sometime later (June 597 seems to be the most likely date)[43] and then not alone but with others, presumably some of his great men and advisors.

42 Ibid., I, 55, 74.
43 Ibid., I, 26, 76. No precise date is given by Bede for the conversion of Ethelbert; for a discussion of the date 597, see Nicholas Brooks, *The Early History of the Church of Canterbury* (Leicester, UK: Leicester University Press, 1984), 8–9.

In Kent, therefore, baptism, marriage, and politics were intimately intertwined: through Bertha, great-granddaughter of Clovis, Ethelbert heard of and learned to respect Christianity, through a marriage primarily undertaken to cement his contacts with Gaul and Rome—a mixture of elements which appears in various ways in the conversion of other Anglo-Saxons.

In Northumbria, a similar situation soon developed: Ethelbert's daughter, Ethelburga, was, like her mother Bertha, a Christian princess who was involved in the conversion of a kingdom. Edwin, the king of Northumbria, sent ambassadors to her brother Eadbald (who had himself been a pagan and had received baptism not long before) to ask for a marriage alliance between the kingdoms. Eadbald insisted that his sister should have full liberty to practice her religion in the pagan court, and accordingly she went north with Bishop Paulinus, one of the second group of monks sent by St. Gregory from Rome, thus introducing Christianity into the northern royal court.[44] As in Kent, foreign alliances and the political motives of kings combined with the presence of a Christian wife, but these were not sufficient for conversion. Edwin, like Ethelbert, allowed the Christians to preach, but did not himself receive baptism until he had conferred with his thanes and obtained their agreement to the change. It is significant that both Bertha and Ethelburga needed to be urged by the pope to try to convert their husbands more firmly; clearly, marriage to a Christian was in itself only a factor towards conversion and should be seen as part of a complex of influences, secular and sacred.[45]

The importance of consultation before a king's conversion is brought out in the situation of Redwald, king of East Anglia. Redwald received

---

44 *EHEP*, Bk. 2, 9, 162.
45 Ibid., 2, 11, 172–74, for the letter of Pope Boniface to Ethelburga. Letter of Pope Gregory to Queen Bertha, Ep. XXIX, in *Epistles of Gregory the Great*, trans. J. Barmby, *Nicene and Post-Nicene Fathers* (Second Series), vol. XIII, Bk. XI, Letter XXIX, 56–57.

baptism alone while he was in Kent during the lifetime of Ethelbert, but when he returned home, he was unable to implement this without the support and agreement of his family and his thanes: "on his return home, he was seduced by his wife and by certain evil teachers and perverted from the sincerity of his faith."[46] He compromised and had a Christian altar alongside a pagan altar in the same building. If Redwald is indeed the king for whom the Sutton Hoo ship-burial was prepared, the artefacts there illustrate this ambivalence.[47]

Later, when Edwin of Northumbria was in exile and as yet unbaptized, he took refuge at the court of Redwald, and Redwald's wife was again influential in persuading her husband to support the young man. The sons of Redwald became Christian: one, Sigebert, incurring his father's anger and fleeing to Gaul, the other, Eorpwald, being persuaded to baptism by Redwald's previous guest, Edwin.

Marriage alliance was linked with conversion and politics in the pagan kingdom of Mercia also. Here, Penda remained a pagan all his life but permitted the preaching of Christianity and indeed was said to dislike nominal Christians: "He hated and despised those who, after they had accepted the Christian faith, were clearly lacking in the works of faith."[48] His daughter Cyneburgh was married to Aldfrid, son of Oswy, the Christian king of Northumbria, a friend of Bishop Wilfrid, and active in Church affairs, for instance at the Council of Whitby.[49] Penda's son, Peada, who was also sub-king under his father in the Midlands, asked for the hand of the Christian princess Alhflaed, the daughter of Oswy and the sister of Aldfrid. Oswy made it a condition

---

46 *EHEP*, Bk. 2, 15, 188–90.
47 The ship-burial at Sutton Hoo has been widely discussed; a thorough analysis can be found in R. L. S. Bruce-Mitford (with others), *The Sutton Hoo Ship-Burial*, 2 vols., 1975, 1978.
48 *EHEP*, Bk. 3, 21, 280.
49 Ibid., Bk. 3, 25, 294–308. For an alternative account of the Council of Whitby, see Eddius Stephanus, "The Life of Wilfrid," trans. J. F. Webb, ed. with introduction by D. H. Farmer, in *The Age of Bede* (London: Penguin Books, 1965).

of the marriage alliance that Peada should become Christian, and Aldfrid, a friend of Peada, "earnestly persuaded" him to do so. Peada was baptized by Bishop Finan "together with all his thanes and gesiths."[50] It seems that Christianity became well-established in Peada's kingdom and flourished particularly under Wulfhere, the younger son of Penda and Peada's successor. It is ironic to note that Peada himself was murdered by his wife, the Christian princess for whom he had accepted Christianity "during the very time of the Easter festival."[51] Presumably her loyalty to her father's house exceeded her loyalty to her husband—an indication, of which there are many in Bede, of the strength of the pagan and political ties above those of the new religion.

In addition to this pattern of conversion through politics and marriage alliances, in which often the kings involved stood godfather to one another, there was the factor of exile. Anglo-Saxon kings ruled smaller or larger groups of men and were continually fighting one another. They were subject also to the blood-feud. In such a situation, in an island newly settled by the invaders and with the unalterable limits of its coast line, it is not surprising that so many of the leaders, and probably lesser men also, spent so much time in exile. Sigebert and Edwin were in exile before they became kings; and at various times Oswald, Owsy, and Aldfrid in Northumbria and Cenwalh and Ceadwalla in Wessex went abroad. When Oswald took over the realm of Northumbria, the queen Edwin had taken from Kent fled back there with her bishop, Paulinus, and thought it prudent to send her children to the court of her friend King Dagobert in Gaul.[52]

Exile ensured that all kings recruited into their service men from other kingdoms; it gave them experience of other and older cultures

50 Ibid., Bk. 3, 21, 278–90.
51 Ibid., Bk. 3, 24, 294.
52 Ibid., Bk. 2, 20, 204. It is clear that Ethelburga placed no reliance on the Christianity of King Oswald, and removed her family before he could destroy them as possible rivals.

than their own, and in many cases it was while they were in exile that they were baptized. Oswald, for instance, one of the sons of King Aethelfrith of Northumbria, spent the whole of the reign of Edwin, Aethelfrith's enemy and successor, in exile with his brothers "among the Irish or the Picts" where, Bede tells us, "they were instructed in the faith as the Irish taught it and were regenerated by the grace of baptism."[53]

This Irish connection was to be as influential in England in the north as was that of Italy and Gaul in the south. Oswald sent for missionaries from Ireland, and eventually Aidan was sent who, with his companions, and in close association with the king, became the apostle of Northumbria. The influence of Irish learning and love of letters came with these monks, just as in the south the school system of Gaul was introduced into East Anglia, where Sigebert, who had been in exile in Gaul because of the enmity of Redwald, had both received baptism and admired the schools: "with the help of Bishop Felix . . . he established a school where boys could be taught letters."[54]

With this story of the enormous vigour and ambition of the Anglo-Saxon kings, with their continual wars and rivalries, their political alliances and inevitable betrayals, their return to paganism and their greed for gold, Bede presents the growth—the amazingly strong and quick growth—of Christianity, gradually penetrating even the warrior ideology, until at the end of his account he could write with something more than rhetorical wishful thinking, "this is the state of the whole of Britain at the present time, about 285 years after the coming of the Anglo-Saxons to Britain, in the year of our Lord 731. Let the earth rejoice in his perpetual kingdom and let Britain rejoice in his faith and let the multitude of the isles be glad and give thanks at the remembrance of his holiness."[55]

53   Ibid., Bk. 3, 1, 212.
54   Ibid., Bk. 3, 18, 268.
55   Ibid., Bk. 5, 23, 560.

For Bede one sign of the thorough conversion of the English was the fact that many of the "both noble and simple have laid aside their weapons and taken the tonsure, preferring that they and their children should take monastic vows rather than train themselves in the art of war."[56] Many pages of the *Ecclesiastical History* are concerned with monks: the Irish at Iona and Lindisfarne, at Whitby and Lastingharn, and the Roman monks at Canterbury, Ripon, and Jarrow. Monks came from Rome and monks from Ireland, and combined their influence with that of monastic Gaul, where some Britons had gone, since they could not find monastic training initially in England. The Irish monks, such as Aidan and Columba and Chad, were highly respected for their austerity and zeal; the Roman monks, such as Augustine, Mellitus, Laurence, Justus, and later the Greek Theodore, for their life of ordered prayer and worship.

The influence of the kings was as important to the establishment of monastic life as it was to conversion. At Canterbury, the Abbey of St. Peter and St. Paul (now St. Augustine's) was the burial place of the kings of Kent; in the north, the abbey at Whitby was the sepulchre of the royalty of Northumbria.[57] Kings sometimes renounced their authority for the cloister and queens and princesses frequently became nuns.[58] The best known of these is Hilda, a princess of Deira, and cousin of King Edwin; her sister became queen of the East Angles, and Hilda was succeeded as abbess of Whitby by Elfleda, the daughter of its founder Oswy.[59] Jarrow, Bede's own monastery, was founded by Benedict Biscop, a Northumbrian nobleman and a retainer of Oswy. At twenty-five he obtained a land grant from the king and began to travel widely

---

56 Ibid.
57 Ibid., Bk. 3, 24, 292, for the burial of Edwin at Whitby; cf. *The Earliest Life of Gregory the Great* by an Anonymous Monk of Whitby, ed. and trans. B. Colgrave (Cambridge, UK: Cambridge University Press, 1985), 104.
58 *EHEP*, Bk. 3, 28, 266–68.
59 Ibid., Bk. 4, 23, 404–14.

abroad, becoming a monk and eventually building the monasteries of Wearmouth and Jarrow, filling them with treasures from Rome and Gaul, and above all with the books which gave Bede the opportunity to become the greatest scholar of his age.[60]

With such involvement of the aristocracy in monastic life, a tension of ideals was set up which Bede himself noted and deplored. In the *Ecclesiastical History* he underlines this tension in, for instance, a story of Bishop Aidan and King Oswin, the unfortunate brother of Oswy, who was murdered by his most Christian brother's orders. Oswin gave Aidan a horse, in the traditional manner of an Anglo-Saxon king, the gift-giver, whose favour was given along with the gift. Aidan, a monk, with very different patterns of behaviour in mind, gave the king's gift to a beggar. The king protested, and Aidan defended his action in the great hall, where the king "who had just come in from hunting stood warming himself by the fire with his thanes," emphasizing the unimportance of worldly goods and kingly patronage compared to the needs of the poor. The story, as vivid as possible from the hands of such a superb storyteller as Bede, concludes with the realization by the king of this different scale of values. "At once he took off his sword and gave it to a thane and hastening to where the bishop sat, threw himself at his feet and asked his pardon."[61] Bede ends the story with a touch which contains a wealth of social comment: Aidan began to weep while the king went back to sit down to the feast, and when another Irishman asked him (in Celtic) why, he said, "I know that the king will not live long, for I never saw before a humble king."[62]

The tensions involved between monastic values and those of a warrior class were not always so simply resolved. Bede also tells the

---

60 Benedict Biscop's life is described by Bede in *The Lives of the Abbots of Wearmouth and Jarrow*, trans. J. F. Webb, in *The Age of Bede*, ed.Farmer, 185–211.
61 *EHEP*, Bk. 3, 14, 258.
62 Ibid.

story of Sigebert, the son of Redwald, who was baptized while in exile in Gaul. He resigned his office as king and became a monk. When Penda of Mercia attacked East Anglia, his countrymen asked Sigebert to return and help fight the pagan king; Sigebert refused and was dragged unwillingly to the field of battle, where he was killed and the army destroyed.[63] Bede does not comment favourably on this, and it seems that here he deplores the failure of a king in not doing the proper work of a king, in contrast to Oswald, the saintly king of Northumbria whom Bede presents as a great war leader and also a Christian saint who died willingly in battle at the hands of the same enemy.[64]

Bede was himself a monk and therefore had no illusions about the value of monastic life in itself; and it is not surprising to find, in his letter to Egbert, that he wrote with despondency about the many English monasteries of his day which were aristocratic clubs rather than strongholds of the life of the spirit.[65]

Bede stresses the importance for the conversion of the Anglo-Saxons of the interpenetration of Christian values and the structures of aristocratic society, yet he himself found the social structure of little lasting value. As a monk, this greatest of the historians of the conversion of a barbarian nation was not interested in barbarians; he was interested in their end—that is, the kingdom of heaven. It is tempting, however, to see Bede too much as a Doctor of the Church, a man whose greatness and goodness is trans-temporal and immediate, and also as a historian who would be entirely at home with modern critical study of texts. This view has its value, but it is instructive to look also at Bede in his own day, a man within his own times and of those times. We know

---

63   Ibid., Bk. 3, 28, 266–68.
64   Ibid., Bk. 3, 2, 214–18.
65   Letter to Egbert, archbishop of York, by Bede, trans. D. Whitelock, in *English Historical Documents*, vol. 1, c. 500–1042 (London, 1955). For an instance of the decline in monastic standards see *EHEP* IV, 25, 420–26, in the case of the nuns of Coldingham.

Bede through his own many writings, through his own account of himself, through the comments of contemporaries, and especially in an account of his death drawn by an intimate disciple. He was born in 672 in Northumbria, just after the death of Oswy, while Theodore was archbishop of Canterbury and Wilfrid was pursuing his tempestuous career at York, and when even Mercia could boast of a Christian king. He says nothing of his parents, and this is in accord with his conviction as a monk that earthly parentage is of no importance compared with life in the kingdom.[66] He was given as a child to the monastery of Jarrow, newly founded by Benedict Biscop as a twin monastery with the monastery of St. Peter at Wearmouth, and spent all his life there: "From that time I spent all the days of my life in the said monastery," until he died sixty-three years old in 735.[67] The offering of small children to monasteries was a common practice and one which is mentioned more than once in the *Eccesiastical History*, most strikingly perhaps in the case of Elfleda, the daughter of King Oswy, who was dedicated by her father at the age of one ("scarcely a year old") in the monastery of Hartlepool where Hilda was abbess, as a thanksgiving for his victory in the battle of Winwaed.[68] The anonymous account of the *Lives of the Abbots* of Bede's monastery mentions a small boy who, with the Abbot Ceolfrid, alone survived a severe onslaught of the plague there, and it may be that this boy was Bede.[69] His admiration for Ceolfrid and for the other abbots is apparent in Bede's own *Lives of the Abbots*.[70]

It is unlikely that Bede ever went further from his monastery than Lindisfarne and possibly York; he never became an abbot or bishop

---

66 Cf. H. Mayr-Harting, "The Venerable Bede: The Rule of St Benedict and Social Class," Jarrow Lecture, 1976.
67 *EHEP*, Bk. 5, 24, 566.
68 Ibid., Bk. 3, 24, 290–92.
69 *History of the Abbots* by an anonymous author, Latin text ed. C. Plummer (1896), cap. xiv., *English Historical Documents*, vol. I, 758–70.
70 Bede, "Lives of the Abbots of Wearmouth and Jarrow," trans. J. F. Webb, in *The Age of Bede*, ed. Farmer, 185–211.

and had no direct influence on church or state. He described his own life thus: "I spent all the days of my life in the said monastery, applying all my study to the meditation of holy Scripture and observing the discipline of the rule and the daily task of singing in the church; it has always been my delight to learn or to teach or to write."[71]

The monk Cuthbert who wrote an account of Bede's death assures us that his concern for his pupils continued when he was dying—he occupied his last days in completing a translation of St. John's Gospel into English, a noteworthy part of his concern with those of the English who did not know Latin, and with a selection of passages from Isidore's *On the Wonders of Nature*, the most influential book for natural history in the early Middle Ages, because, he said, "I cannot have my children learning what is not true, and losing their labour on this after I have gone."[72]

Bede was known in his own time as a great commentator on the Scriptures, and clearly that is how he wished to be known—his commentaries drew together those of the Latin Fathers of the Church in a "library of the fathers," and Bede expanded them with his own allegorical interpretations of the Scriptures. In this he was of his own time and in the tradition of St. Augustine and St. Gregory the Great, to whom he constantly refers. Of his own times, also, were his books on chronology, which remained the classic authority in Europe until the sixteenth century. Even today we feel the influence of Bede as a chronologer since he adopted and made fashionable our present calculation of years within the Christian era, but it is also true to say that the kind of calculations involved were of more interest to his contemporaries than to ourselves.

To stand in the ruins of the monastery of Jarrow today is to be far from the world of Bede, further than when reading his works. The

---

71 *EHEP*, Bk. 5, 24, 566.
72 "Cuthbert's Letter on the Death of Bede," *EHEP*, 580–86.

once-busy monastery—with its rich endowments and the spoils of the Mediterranean world in its walls and windows, in its ornaments and in its library, open to the visits of kings, open also to the poor, full of news of the world from visitors who generally found their way to the cell of Bede—this lively monastery is reduced to silent stones in a grey landscape with industrial Yorkshire on the horizon. Bede died there on the Vigil of Ascension Day, a contented man: "I have not lived so that life among you now would make me ashamed, but I am not afraid to die either, for the God we serve is good."[73] "Not afraid to die": that is to come to the place which Augustine of Hippo recommended to his dying friend Nebridius. "There is need of much withdrawal of oneself from the tumult of the things that are passing away in order that there may be formed in man . . . the ability to say, 'I fear nought.'"[74]

This peace of heart fills that *Ecclesiastical History* which Bede wrote towards the end of his life, placing the rivalries, political machinations, greed, valour, and tumult of the Anglo-Saxon kings and nobles within the light of the coming of the kingdom of God; it shows up their limitations, and it shows even more the working of the mercy of God within those limitations. At the end of the book, the most vivid of all accounts of a barbarian society in the process of conversion, Bede added his own prayer, as the heir of this tale of nobility, treachery, and conversion:

> And I pray thee, merciful Jesus, that as thou hast graciously granted me sweet draughts from the Word which tells of Thee, so wilt Thou of Thy goodness, grant that I may come at length to Thee, the fount of all wisdom, and stand before Thy face forever. Here, with God's help, ends the fifth book of the *History of the English Church*.[75]

73 Ibid., 582.
74 *Letters of St Augustine of Hippo*, X, Letter to Nebridius, trans. M. Dods (Edinburgh, 1872), 24.
75 *EHEP*, Bk. 5, 24, 570.

3

BEDE
and THE PSALTER

Lord, what love have I unto Thy law;
all the day long is my study in it.
(Ps. 119:97)

D
uring Bede's last illness his constant companion, the monk
Cuthbert, noted that after giving daily lessons to his pupils
Bede would spend "the rest of the day chanting the psalter as
best he could".[76] Other saints have also died with the psalms as the basis
of their prayer: Augustine, for instance, in the fourth century, had the
seven penitential psalms always before him, and Teresa of Avila in the
sixteenth century repeated over and over again the verse from Psalm
51, "A broken and a contrite heart, O God, thou wilt not despise."

The hundred and fifty psalms of the Old Testament have always
had a central place in the tradition of Christian prayer, but it is not
immediately clear why that collection of Jewish prayers and poems
should be words for Christians to live and die by. The Jewish psalter
was naturally the prayer book of Jesus and the apostles, but it became
the prayer of the early Church in spite of, rather than because of, its
Jewish roots. The psalms were composed by David, who was the
ancestor of Christ, and each was therefore seen as a particular
prophecy of Christ. Paul recommended the Christians in Ephesus

76 *Epistola de Obitu Bedae*, in Bede, *Ecclesiastical History of the English People*, ed.
and trans. B. Colgrave and R. A. B. Mynors (Oxford, 1969), p. 581.

and Colosse to celebrate their redemption "in psalms and hymns and spiritual songs" (Eph. 5:9; Col. 3:6) because already they were redolent for them with the good news of Christ, but these reasons for love of the psalms are not the most vital. The basic reason why it is the psalms that strengthen dying men is surely that the evangelists, in recording how Christ on the Cross used the words of Psalm 22, "My God, my God, why hast thou forsaken me," and for his ultimate prayer, Psalm 30, "Father, into thy hands I commend my spirit" (Luke 23:34 and 46), adduced the highest possible instance of their use.

The psalms have been used by Christians in three principal ways, and Bede was concerned with each of them. First of all, there is the public, corporate recitation of the psalms, as praise and adoration, as repentance, intercession, and petition, which the Church, the body of Christ, offers to the Father, that sacrifice of praise to which Benson of Cowley gave the title "The War Songs of the Prince of Peace." Secondly, there is the scholarly, academic approach to the psalter which is concerned with the words themselves. And thirdly, there is personal meditation on the psalms in the long tradition of *compunctio cordis*, that bright sorrow without which Christianity is merely a religion and a rite. The use of the psalms in the liturgy shaped Bede's mind throughout his life more consistently than any other text, and in both scholarship and in prayer he made major contributions to their use.

The Psalter and the Liturgy

The psalms were used in public corporate worship from the earliest times,[77] those psalms which were appropriate being selected for prayer at the beginning and ending of the day. John Chrysostom, bishop of Constantinople and the focal point of the liturgical life of its church in

---

77 For a summary of evidence about Christian customs of prayer in the first
    centuries, see P. Salmon, *Les Tituli Psalmorum des Manuscrits Latins* (Rome
    1959), pp. 10–11, and R. Taft, *The Liturgy of the Hours in East and West*
    (Collegeville, MN: Liturgical Press, 1986), pp. 3–11.

the fourth century, recommended the psalms for all times and occasions in a lively sermon, with the refrain: "first, last, and central is David":

> If we keep vigil in the church, David comes first, last and central. If early in the morning we chant songs and hymns, first, last and central is David again. If we are occupied with the funeral solemnities of those who have fallen asleep, David is first, last and central.

Not only in the solemn liturgies of the great church, he says, but in all gatherings of Christians, learned or otherwise, the psalter is central:

> O amazing wonder! Many who have made little progress in literature know the psalter by heart. Nor is it only in cities and churches that David is famous, in the village market, in the desert, in uninhabitable land or if girls sit at home and spin, he excites the praises of God.

Clearly, he is talking about all the holy people of God in their ordinary ways of life, not the specialist category of monks, for he then goes on to mention them:

> In the monasteries, among those holy choirs of angelic armies, David is first, last and central. In convents of virgins, where are the communities of those who imitate Mary, in deserts where there are men crucified to the world, who live their life in heaven with God, David is first, last and central. All other men at night are asleep, David alone is active, and gathering the saints of God into seraphic bands, he turns earth into heaven and converts men into angels.[78]

---

78 John Chrysostom, Panegyric on the psalter, in *The Holy Psalter*, ed. L. Moore, (Madras, 1966), p. xxv.

For the whole Church, the psalms were uniquely prized, and, like all Scripture, they were seen as more than human words, for in them God spoke through David as a prophet of Christ. In various ways the liturgy indicated to believers that the Jewish psalms were illuminated by the light of Christ falling upon their pages. The liturgical year itself gave new meaning to the same psalm as it was selected on different occasions: for instance, the verse from Psalm 24, "Lift up your heads, O ye gates, and be ye lift up ye everlasting doors, for the King of Glory shall come in," takes on a new meaning whether it is sung at Christmas, to signify the entry of the Lord into the world; at Easter, to signify his descent into hell; or at Ascension, to signify his entry into the gates of heaven.

The addition of other words could also interpret a psalm, the simplest being the conclusion of each psalm with the words: "Glory be to the Father, and to the Son, and to the Holy Spirit," directing the prayer to the Trinity. Antiphons—phrases sung either before or during the chanting of the psalm—served to bring out the Christological significance of the psalm. Collects also interpreted the words of each psalm; these were prayers read at the conclusion of a psalm or group of psalms to direct prayer towards Christ.[79] A text which combines the liturgical use of Psalm 24 with both antiphons and prayers is the one which Bede sang in his last illness:

> O King of Glory, Lord of Might, who didst this day ascend in triumph above all the heavens, leave us not comfortless, but send to us the Spirit of the Father, even the Spirit of Truth. Alleluia.[80]

From the beginning of his life at Wearmouth, Bede heard the psalms sung by his brothers, and he set himself the task of learning them by heart. When he joined Ceolfrith at the newly founded monastery of St.

---

79 Cf. L. Brou and A. Wilmart, *The Psalter Collects from V and VI Century Sources,* vol. 83 (London: Henry Bradshaw Society, 1949).
80 *Epistola de Obitu Bedae,* op. cit., p. 583.

Paul at Jarrow, he found that Ceolfrith had established there "the same complete method of chanting and reading which was maintained in the older monastery," although not all the twenty-two members were able to chant or read in church. Four years later, Bede, competent in both chanting and reading, had vivid experience of the importance of the tradition of the Christological interpretation of the psalter, if, as I think most probable, Bede is to be identified as the boy who survived the plague of 686 with Ceolfrith:

In the monastery over which Ceolfrith presided, all those brethren who could read or preach or recite the antiphons and responds were taken away, with the exception of the abbot and one little lad who had been reared and taught by him, and who is at this time still in the same monastery where he holds the rank of priest and both by written and spoken words justly commends his teacher's praiseworthy acts to all who desire to know of them. Now he (I mean the abbot) being much distressed by reason of the aforesaid pestilence, gave command that, their former use being suspended, they should go through the whole psalter, except at matins and vespers, without the recitation of the antiphons. And when this practice had been followed not without many tears and lamentation on his part for the space of one week, being unable to endure it any longer he resolved once again that the customary order of the psalms with their antiphons should be restored.[81]

"Tears" and "lamentation" indicate considerable distress, and I do not suppose that Ceolfrith was so upset at having to omit the antiphons simply because the Offices sounded more impressive when sung in full,

---

81 *Life of Ceolfrith, Abbot of Wearmouth and Jarrow*, trans. D. S. Boutflower (London, 1912), cap. 4, p. 65.

nor out of a legalistic sense that everything must be said. It was, after all, perfectly acceptable to simplify the Office in this way, and such a practice was recommended in the Rule of St. Benedict. The words of this account convey a sense of intolerable loss, which surely must have come from the absence of the antiphons whose words made the psalms into Christian prayers. Ceolfrith's devotion to the psalter was outstanding even for his own times: at Jarrow he recited the psalter twice daily in addition to the Offices, and on his last journey to Rome he "daily chanted the psalter of David in order three times over."[82] For him as a Christian, the psalms were the basic scaffolding for all his prayer. His influence on Bede was profound in this matter of the psalms, no less than in scriptural commentary and in doctrine.

The story of Ceolfrith and the boy Bede indicates that the psalms were used with antiphons at Jarrow in Bede's time. There is no direct information about the Office at Wearmouth-Jarrow before or during Bede's life. There are, however, certain influences that can be conjectured: the first is the Office as prescribed for other monastic houses, perhaps especially that outlined in the Rule of St. Benedict. It is tempting to cut the Gordian knot and assume that Benedict Biscop and Ceolfrith used the complex arrangement of the psalms for the Office according to the Rule of St. Benedict, but there is little evidence, apart from the respect shown by Bede for certain chapters of the Rule,[83] that it was any more than one rule among many which the abbots drew upon to organise life in the new monasteries. Moreover, the arrangement of psalmody in the Rule of St. Benedict was something left specifically to the discretion of the abbot.[84] Ceolfrith was well acquainted with the custom at Ripon where, according to Eddius Stephanus, Wilfrid

---

82 Ibid., cap. 33, p. 81.

83 Cf. H.M.R.E. Mayr-Harting, *The Venerable Bede, the Rule of St Benedict, and Social Class,* Jarrow Lecture, 1976.

84 *Rule of St. Benedict,* cap. 18, "We strongly recommend, if this arrangement of the psalms be displeasing to anyone, that he arrange them otherwise."

had introduced the Rule of St. Benedict, which required monks to be instructed in how to "make use of a double choir singing in harmony, with reciprocal responses and antiphons."[85] But Ceolfrith had begun his monastic experience in the Irish monastery of Gilling, and also knew the monastery of Botolf in Suffolk and another monastery in Kent, while Benedict Biscop knew the Offices at the monastery of Lérins, and at St. Peter's Canterbury as well as at the various monasteries and churches of Rome. Just how distinct the Offices in these places were from the Office in the Rule of St. Benedict at that period is not clear, but it seems safe to assume that the whole psalter was recited each week, the major part of it at the Office of Vigils during the night.

The Offices at Wearmouth, whatever they had been like at the monastery's foundation, were further shaped by the customs of seventh-century Rome. In 679 Benedict Biscop and Ceolfrith had visited Rome together, and there Pope Agatho had agreed to allow John, the precentor of St. Peter's and abbot of the monastery of St. Martin, to "teach the monks of [their] monastery the mode of chanting throughout the year as it was practised at St. Peter's in Rome."[86] The cantors of the monastery therefore learned the distribution of the psalms; the order and manner of singing and reading aloud; the lessons and texts of the antiphons and responds; and the cycle of feasts in use at St. Peter's.[87] They learned not so much from books as from a performer, and among the children of the monastery who heard him at that time was Bede, who entered the monastery in 680, the same year that John came to Wearmouth. By the time he went to Jarrow, he knew the psalter and was well able, unlike some others, to practise this new method of

---

85 Eddius Stephanus, *Life of Bishop Wilfrid*, ed. and trans. B. Colgrave (Cambridge, 1927), cap. LXVII, p. 99.
86 Bede, *Ecclesiastical History*, op. cit., Bk. IV, cap. xviii, p. 389.
87 "They brought back with them to Britain John (of blessed memory), precentor of the church in Rome, who taught us abundantly the systematic rule of chanting, both by his own living voice and from the musical score." *Life of Ceolfrith*, op. cit. cap. 10, p. 62.

chant. The basilica of St. Peter was the focus of the devotion of pilgrims and especially of the Anglo-Saxons, and the founders of Wearmouth-Jarrow could find no better model for their own devotions.

The Office at St. Peter's, which John brought to the north, had been established in the second half of the seventh century. It was above all an audible Office, based on Scripture. This Roman tradition of chanting the psalms so that they could be heard and understood spread widely, and later could be insisted upon as the true norm. At the Council of Cloveshoe, for instance, one chapter insisted that the psalter should not be sung "to the tragic tone of the poets" but straightforwardly "according to the Roman use," while another explained in detail the obligation upon monks and clergy to base their worship directly upon the psalter.[88] In Bede's homilies there are references to this custom of chanting psalms and scriptural canticles through the night at vigils, especially at Easter and other great feasts where the psalms were interspersed with Scripture readings. In a sermon for the dedication of a church he writes:

> We traditionally spend the night vigil joyfully singing additional psalms and hearing a large number of lessons, in a church where many lights are burning and the walls are adorned more lavishly than usual.[89]

Canticles—other sections of biblical material arranged for singing—were also included in the rest of the Office; for instance, it is clear from one of Bede's homilies on the Virgin Mary that the Magnificat was sung at Vespers:

---

88 Canons of the Synod of Cloveshoe, 747, in *Councils and Ecclesiastical Documents Relating to Great Britain and Ireland*, ed. A. W. Haddan and W. Stubbs (Oxford, 1871), vol. 111, cap. 2, p. 366, and cap. 27, pp. 372–4.

89 Bede, Homily Bk. 2, 25, *In Dedicatione Ecclesiae*, in *Bedae Venerabilis Homiliarum Evangelii*, ed. D. Hurst, Corpus Christianorum Series Latina CXXII (Turnhout, 1955), p. 368.

It has become an excellent and salutary custom in the church for everyone to sing this hymn (the Magnificat) daily in the Office of evening prayer.[90]

Bede also commented on the canticle of Habakkuk,[91] another text used in the Office, and here his interpretation of the words was also predominantly Christological.

How were these psalms and canticles sung? Presumably, with the single voice of a trained cantor for the psalms, with the repetitive sentences of antiphons as a chorus, either at the beginning and end or repeated after each or several verses. Aethelwulf, describing the chanting a century later in a cell of the monastery of Lindisfarne, says of Siwine, the fifth abbot, that

> when the reverend festivals of God's saints came round and when between two choirs in the church he sang the verses of the psalms among the brothers, they rendered in song the sweet sounding music of the flowing antiphon; and the lector, a man very learned in books, poured forth song to the general delight, singing in a clear voice.[92]

Psalmody was not a new tradition in Bede's day in England; when Augustine came to Kent, he and his companions met in the church of St. Martin to "chant the psalms" first, and then to "pray, to say mass, to preach and to baptise";[93] Aidan and his companions "occupied

---

90 Ibid., Homily Bk. 1, 4, p. 30. This is of special interest in determining when the Magnificat began to be sung at evening prayer; the Eastern Churches include it among the odes at Orthos in the morning; the Rule of St. Benedict recommends a Gospel canticle at Vespers, but this could be the Nunc Dimittis, as in the Eastern tradition.

91 *Expositio Bedae Presbyteri in Canticum Abacuc Prophetae*, ed. J. E. Hudson, Corpus Christianorum Series Latina CXIXb (Turnhout, 1983), pp. 381–409. "It is the custome . . . to sing it each week solemnly at the Morning Office" (p. 381).

92 Aethelwulf, *De Abbatibus*, ed. A. Campbell (Oxford, 1967), cap. 15, p. 40.

93 Bede, *Ecclesiastical History*, op. cit., Bk.1, cap. xxvi, p. 77.

themselves either with reading the Scriptures or learning the psalms."[94]
It is no wonder that Bede, their historian and heir, placed the psalms at
the heart of his life in "the daily task (cura) of singing in the church."[95]

Bede as a Scholar and the Psalms

Bede had, then, a thorough knowledge of the psalms, and in their
Christological aspect they formed the structure of his thought. The
psalter was central for him in solitary prayer as well as in the daily
Offices because it spoke about Christ. For him it was natural to learn
the psalter by heart, one psalm learned and repeated after another:
in this he and Ceolfrith were typical rather than exceptional. Wilfrid
also had learned the whole psalter by heart at Lindisfarne, in the old
version of Jerome; he was able to change the entire mental structure of
his prayer when he was in Rome by learning by heart a second psalter,
that of Jerome's *iuxta hebraicos*.[96] It says much for his powerful intellect
that he could do so. Bede also used the same two psalters, presumably
both known by heart. As a child he was taught the Gallican psalter,
Jerome's first revision of the Latin psalter and the one used in church,
and it was this that he quoted in his writings and which he also used in
his *De Metris et Tropis*. On two occasions, however, he used Jerome's
later version, made from the Hebrew—once for scholarly purposes and
once for prayer. One manuscript of the psalter of very great, indeed
unique, importance was transcribed during Bede's lifetime in his
monastery at Jarrow. This is the *Codex Amiatinus*, the oldest extant
copy of Jerome's complete Vulgate Bible, which has for its version of
the psalms the third revision of Jerome, *iuxta hebraicos*.[97] The three
great pandects made at Jarrow under Ceolfrith may well have owed

---

94 Ibid., Bk. III, cap. V, p. 227.
95 Ibid., Bk. V, cap. 24, p. 267.
96 Eddius Stephanus, op. cit., cap. 2, p. 7; cap. 3, p. 9.
97 *Biblia Sacra Iuxta Vulgatam Versionem* (Stuttgart, 1983), vol. 1, for the Jerome
    psalters *iuxta LXX* and *iuxta hebraicum* compared.

their text to Bede's scholarly eye; certainly his care for Jerome's text *iuxta hebraicos* was in line with the text of the psalter produced for that book. The author of the *Life of Ceolfrith* refers to one of these Bibles as "the pandect which I mentioned derived from its Hebrew and Greek originals by the translations of Jerome the priest."[98]

The form of the Jarrow Bible belongs to the tradition of the *Codex Grandior* of Cassiodorus, but it was "the new translation" that formed the text.[99] Ceolfrith added these "three new copies of the new translation of the Bible" to his library. Perhaps it was Bede the scholar, who most of all delighted in this new text "according to the Hebrew" especially for the psalter, who suggested this change. These books were not after all meant for use when singing in church but for consultation at other times:

> He (Ceolfrith) caused three Pandects to be transcribed, two of which he placed in his two monasteries in their churches in order that all who wished to read any chapter of either Testament might readily find what they desired.[100]

Whether or not Bede had seen a Bible connected with the name of Cassiodorus,[101] he knew very well his commentary on the psalms. He had other commentaries to hand, certainly those of Jerome and Augustine, and as a scholar "following in the footsteps of the Fathers" he used them to further his understanding of the psalms. Their brilliant analysis of the words of the psalms in which they explored every shade of meaning, grammatical as well as spiritual, did as much to colour Bede's understanding of each verse as did the liturgy. Bede

---

98 *Life of Ceolfrith* op. cit. cap. 37, p. 84.
99 Bede, *Lives of the Abbots,* trans. D. H. Farmer, in *The Age of Bede* (Harmondsworth, 1965), cap. 15, p. 201.
100 *Life of Ceolfrith,* op. cit., cap. 20, p. 69.
101 Cf. R. L. S. Bruce-Mitford, *The Art of the Codex Amiatinus,* Jarrow Lecture, 1967, and R. N. V. Bailey, *The Durham Cassiodorus,* Jarrow Lecture, 1978.

never claimed to have made a commentary on the psalter himself, and in the *Tituli Psalmorum* which is attributed to him, it is Cassiodorus who is his main source.[102]

There was another text in which Bede the scholar explored the psalms; this was *De Metris et Tropis*[103] in which Bede, who called learning and prayer "my delight," made the psalms a delight in another way also. For Bede the psalms were prayer and prophecy, but they were also poetry, and poetry as great or greater than any of the classical pagan poets. In *De Metris et Tropis,* Bede used verses from the psalms to illustrate his conviction that they contained examples of all the classical metres of poetry and in a finer way than in any secular verse. There was no need, he said, for the English Christians to pluck the rose of doctrine from among the thorns of the pagan poetry; the psalms of David, the sweet singer of Israel, offered examples as great.[104]

Bede and the Tradition of compunctio cordis in the Psalms

Knowledge of the psalms was integral to Bede's daily work as a monk, and as a scholar he subjected the text of the psalms to constant exploration; but there is a third way in which Bede both used the psalms and influenced their use. This arose specifically out of the context of his life as a monk, and out of the interior aspect of prayer known in the monastic tradition as "compunction."

In the desert of Egypt, among the first Christian monks in that explosion of ascetic life in the fourth century, the psalter was used as the basis of prayer in a special way. Here, two things are evident: first, the psalter was learned aurally by men for the most part unable to read and without books; it was learned by heart, and therefore the

---

102 For discussion of the material in *De Titulis Psalmorum,* see B. Fischer, "Bedae de Titulis psalmorum liber," in *Festschrift Bernhard Bischoff,* ed. J. Autenrieth (Stuttgart, 1971), pp. 90–100.

103 Bede, *De Arte Metrica et de Schematibus Tropis,* ed. C. B. Kendall, Corpus Christianorum Series Latina CXXIIA (Turnhout, 1975), pp. 66–171.

104 Ibid., pp. 142–43.

obvious way to memorise it was to recite one psalm after another. And secondly, because the monks were not performing a ritual which changed with every liturgical season as in a church, but were following a life of prayer in their cells, the interiorisation of the psalms was as natural as breathing, so much so that they tended to despise the Offices and the commentaries used elsewhere:

> The brethren said, "By what means did the fathers sing the psalms of the Holy Spirit without distraction?" The old man said, "First of all they accustomed themselves whenever they stood up to sing the service in their cells, to work carefully at collecting their attention and understanding the meaning of the psalms, and they took care never to let a word escape them without knowing its meaning, not as a mere matter of history, like the interpreters, nor after the manner of the translator like Basil or John Chrysostom, but spiritually according to the interpretation of the fathers, that is to say they applied all the psalms to their own lives and works and to their passions and to their inner life and to the war that the devil waged against them."[105]

The monks said the psalms over and over again, not just at set times; when Bishop Epiphanius, for example, heard of some monks saying the psalms only at the third, sixth, and ninth hours, he said, "The true monk should have prayer and psalmody always in his heart."[106] The psalms were an authentic way into prayer, but they were not for the monks prayer itself; they were a gateway into the life of prayer which is heaven. True prayer, they said, was beyond the repetition of the words of the psalter:

---

105 *The Paradise or Garden of the Holy Fathers*, trans. E. A. W. Budge (London, 1907), vol. 2, p. 306.
106 *Sayings of the Desert Fathers*, trans. Benedicta Ward SLG (Mowbray, 1975), Epiphanius 3.

A monk who has begun to sing the psalms ... with understanding and meditation, may refrain from the psalm and sing a song which is beyond the body and which is the song of the angels.[107]

When Abba Macarius went to pray with two young monks, they recited the psalms until he saw the prayer of fire—that is, the Holy Spirit—come down on one of them.[108]

Abba Lot said to Abba Joseph, 'Abba, as far as I can, I say my little office . . . what else can I do?' Then the old man stood up and stretched his hands towards heaven. His fingers became like ten lamps of fire and he said to him, 'If you will, you can become all flame'.[109]

It is not the grammatical exegesis of Jerome, the doctrinal interpretations of Augustine, or Cassiodorus's combination of both that is most apparent in Bede's use of the psalms in his writings. While there is always good reason to look seriously at Bede's use of the Bible and to unpack the layers of meaning underlying his choice of quotations, this is especially so when he quotes the psalms. Although he had in his mind the commentaries of his predecessors, the various texts of the psalms, and their liturgical use in church, when he quoted a psalm in his writings—where quotations from the psalms more than any other part of Scripture mingle with the text—it was very often not the Christological meaning nor the moral meaning of a verse that Bede drew out, but its precise application to contemporary life.

For Bede the whole Bible was by one author, God, and the psalms were relayed by one author, David, but they were not an end in themselves; through them, God spoke to Christians now, the living word of

---

107 *Paradise of the Fathers,* op. cit., p. 306.
108 *Sayings of the Desert Fathers,* op. cit., Macarius 33.
109 Ibid., Joseph of Panephysis 7.

God clarifying the present and illuminating the one praying. In this he was closer to the monastic hermit tradition of Egypt, and it is the Second Conference of Abba Isaac about prayer, as recorded by John Cassian, which best describes Bede's instinctive use of the psalms. In chapter eleven, when Isaac is explaining the heights of prayer, he uses a verse of psalm 103 about prayer and the psalms: "the high hills are a refuge for the wild goats and so are the stony rocks for the coneys." The translation of the Hebrew *shaphan,* the hiders, has given scope for many translations: in the Greek Septuagint they are badgers, or rock-badgers, the Syrian versions have hyrax or marmot, while the English identify them as coneys or rabbits.[110] But Cassian, like Cassiodorus, in the Latin tradition has *erinaciis,* hedgehogs: the monk who prays the psalms, he says, becomes a sort of spiritual hedgehog, and is continually protected by the shield of the rock of the Gospel:

> This hedgehog of prayer will then take into himself all the thoughts of the psalms and will begin to sing them in such a way that he will utter them with the deepest emotion of his heart . . . as if they were his very own prayer . . . and will take them as aimed at himself and will recognise that their words were not only fulfilled by or in the person of the prophet but that they are fulfilled and carried out daily in his own case.[111]

This hedgehog style of prayer was how Bede used the psalms. Two examples must suffice. At the conclusion of his account of the life and death of Cuthbert of Lindisfarne, Bede quotes Herefrith's description of the chanting of Psalm 59, "O God thou hast cast us out and scattered us abroad," by the brothers on Farne as part of the

---

110 "Coney" from *cuniculus,* as in *Fabula de Petro Cuniculo.*
111 John Cassian, "Second Conference of Abba Isaac," in *Conferences,* trans. E. C. S. Gibson, *Nicene and Post-Nicene Fathers* (Second Series), reprint 1973, cap. XI, p. 408.

ordinary course of the chanting of the psalter at the night office. The psalm was a natural part of the sequence of psalms chanted one after the other at vigils for that night, and Bede was well aware of this and of the interpretations of his predecessors. For Cassiodorus, this psalm was a description of how God had shattered the pride of those bound in sins and would recall them into a strong city which was Christ.[112] For Augustine, the casting out and scattering abroad could apply to any temporal suffering endured for Christ, but was especially appropriate to that of the martyrs.[113] But for Bede what was worth recording in detail was how the context of contemporary events was lit up by the phrases of the psalm, illuminating daily experience in Northumbria in his own time.

After Cuthbert's death, there was trouble at Lindisfarne, such trouble that it could be expressed only in these words of despair, "O God, thou hast cast us out and scattered us abroad." It is not clear why there was such a falling apart, but this text suggests that many monks had left Lindisfarne. Perhaps with the return of the see of Lindisfarne to Bishop Wilfrid, the monastery was afraid it would not prosper; for a year, until a successor was found for Cuthbert, the monastery was again part of Wilfrid's over-large empire. Perhaps the influence of Iona was pulling the place apart. Perhaps the ambiguous nature of the monastery, in which some monks saw themselves as a community and others as disciples of a holy man, was a cause of their falling apart on the death of Cuthbert, who had held them together.[114]

Whatever the reasons, the psalm implies that many monks left in distress; it also seems that with the appointment of Eadberht as bishop, a measure of stability returned. "Turn us again," they seem to have been

112 Cassiodorus *Expositio Psalmorum*, ed. M. Adriaen, Corpus Christianorum Series Latina XCVIII–XCVIIII (Turnhout, 1958); 2 vols, vol. 1, pp. 529–37.
113 Augustine, *Exposition on the Psalms*, trans. A. C. Coxe, *Nicene and Post-Nicene Fathers* (Second Series), reprint 1979, vol. VIII, pp. 244–48.
114 Bede, *Life of St Cuthbert*, ed. and trans. B. Colgrave in, *Two Lives of St Cuthbert* (Cambridge, 1940), cap. xi, pp. 285–289.

crying after the death of Cuthbert, and in Bede's lifetime that restoration had happened. The psalm was given an immediate application to human events, rather than a grammatical or Christological meaning. There is a sense of wonder in Bede's account of Herefrith's words, that the psalm should later be seen to have so exactly expressed events and emotions.

Another death also was accompanied by a Psalm which Bede saw as significant, that of his abbot Benedict Biscop, which he described in the *History of the Abbots of Wearmouth and Jarrow.* This was Psalm 82, of which the second verse was to Bede significant: "For lo, thine enemies make a murmuring and they that hate thee have lift up their head." On 12 January, it was being chanted by the brothers in the normal course of the Office in the church at Wearmouth, as the abbot and founder lay dying.[115] Jerome had interpreted this psalm as being about either the Church and heretics or the Israelites and their enemies, actual and spiritual; Cassiodorus found in it a doctrinal meaning about Christ and the soul; for Augustine, it was a psalm concerning the Church and the world, or Christ and evil. But for Bede, its meaning was deeply personal when related to the death of the abbot who had received him into the community. Well aware of previous interpretations of the psalms, he was yet alert to see a vigorous and lively meaning—not antiquarian, not limited by previous commentary—in relation to present events, and was ready to pray the texts in the light of Christ through his own life and experience. And here his insistence on this interpretation shed a discreet light upon the death of Benedict Biscop; it was, says Bede, a prayer for deliverance and protection in extreme danger at death. The cell of the abbot, dying after great suffering, did not contain a peaceful scene such as the death of Caedmon, Drythelm, Boisil, or Bede himself. For this former thane, a much-travelled, energetic, and

---

115 Bede, *History of the Abbots,* op. cit., cap. 14, pp. 199–200.

able man (Bede tells us by his comments on this psalm), death was a
bitter agony of soul as well as body. And Benedict Biscop was no less
a saint for that prolonged anguish, terror, and indignity which all men
fear most in dying.

To use the words of the psalms to articulate present terror and grief,
as well as joy and wonder, is to discover through the psalms hope beyond
hope. As a cry of protest against the inhumanity of man, the words of
the psalms are always especially appropriate. Whether the horror is
personal or cosmic, whether it is Christ on the Cross, genocide among
nations, exile from a monastic home, the loss of someone held dear, or
the personal anguish of the dying, the words of the psalms express that
for which we have no words and at the same time link us into the life of
redeeming love: "Out of the deep have I called unto thee, O Lord, Lord,
hear my voice"; "I am so fast in prison that I cannot get out"; "O deliver
me from them that persecute me for they are too strong for me"; "My
God, my God, why hast thou forsaken me?" Bede commended this use
of the psalms in these words:

> If any oppressive sorrow has come upon you, either by an
> injury brought on by others, or by a besetting fault, or by an
> overwhelming domestic loss, if you grieve for any reason at all, do
> not murmur against one another or place the blame on God, but
> rather pray with psalms to the Lord lest the sadness of the world
> which is death swallow you up; drive the destructive sickness of
> grief from your heart by the frequent sweetness of the psalms.[116]

It would be possible to make a commentary on the psalter out of
Bede's use of the psalms in his writings, and it would be in this mode
of interpretative light shed upon the day-to-day personal experience

---

116 Bede, *Commentary on the Seven Catholic Epistles*, trans. D. Hurst (Collegeville,
  MN: Cistercian Publications, 1985), Commentary on James 5:13, pp. 60–61.

of the one praying. It is this tradition of the use of the psalter as the words through which someone could express his own prayer to Christ, as a means of piercing the heart—compunction—to allow the waters of baptism to flood into the whole person in the present, that Bede inherited, used, and lived by.

The psalms were a structure for personal prayer, but Bede did more than use the psalms in this way: he popularised their use by composing a new kind of prayer from them in his abbreviated psalter.[117] It was not a liturgical psalter he had in mind, and this gave him freedom to choose any version of the psalms he liked. He selected the best text he knew, Jerome's third psalter, *iuxta hebraicos*. From this he selected verses from each psalm which could be used as direct prayer or praise, as food for meditation, plea for mercy, protest, contrition, or adoration and exultation. Sometimes one verse alone was used, sometimes several. The verses were also selected so that a sense of the meaning of the psalm as a whole was retained; it would be possible to recall the whole psalm from these clues.

There is only one psalm which seems not to have been properly represented, and that is, oddly enough, Psalm 136, the great psalm of compunction, *Supra Flumina Babylonis*, "By the waters of Babylon we sat down and wept." The verse which is now included as coming from this psalm is *beatus homo qui amat dominum,* a phrase not found in this psalm nor in the psalter, nor indeed in any version of any book of the Bible which I have yet found, nor in any commentary,

---

117 *Collectio Psalterii Bedae,* ed. J. Fraipont, *Bedae Venerabilis Opera,* Corpus Christianorum Series Latina CXXII (Turnhout, 1955), pp. 452–70. (See the appendix of this chapter for a translation.)
 Three ninth-century manuscripts contain this text:
 a   Paris, Bibl. Nat. Lat. 1153, ff. 56v–65v, written in the Abbey of S. Denis c. 850 (ed. A. Duchesne, PL C1, cols. 569–79).
 b. Paris, Bibl. Nat. Lat. 13.388, from St. Martin of Tours c. 850 (ed. A. Wilmart, *Precum Libelli quattuor Aevi Karolini,* Rome, 1940, pp. 143–159; also E. Martene, PL XCIV, cols. 515–27.)
 c. Koln, Domkappitel 106, ff. 65–71, c. 805.

psalm-collect, or antiphon which I have met. In one of the two early manuscripts which contain the abbreviations, it has been rationalised to *beatus vir qui timet dominum* from Psalm 111, which is no help at all. It is possible that it is the result of a series of copying mistakes of the verse, *beatus qui tenebit et adlidet parvulos tuos ad petram,* "blessed is he that taketh thy children and throweth them against the stones," but the paleographical errors are unlikely and the choice of sentiment even more so, however carefully glossed.[118] With this inexplicable exception, the text is both a compendium of the whole psalter and a key to each psalm, as well as a collection of phrases admirably suited to private and personal prayer.

The *Abbreviations from the Psalter* was a turning point in the history of prayer, providing a vehicle for popular devotion for the next four centuries. The man who was most enthusiastically vocal in his praise of the psalter as a book for prayer was also an Englishman, also from the north; this was Alcuin, a pupil of the school of Egbert, Bede's colleague, at York. Alcuin recommended the psalter earnestly as the basis of intimate prayer, speaking out of the same tradition as Bede, but carrying it into another mode of self-awareness. There is in Alcuin more interior interest in the person praying and his needs, the words of the psalm being seen as the perfect expression of human praise, wonder, love, and delight as well as sorrow, repentance, and at times revolt and protest, though with a strong sense also of the external form of the psalms. In this he belongs to the monastic world, and especially to the tradition of the solitary life, and he expanded and elaborated the way indicated by Bede when he wrote:

> In the psalms if you look carefully you will find an intimacy
> of prayer such as you could never discover by yourself. In the
> psalms you will find an intimate confession of your sins, and

118 I am indebted to Dom Maurice Bogaert of the Abbey of Maredsous for useful
    suggestions on this matter.

a perfect supplication for divine mercy. In the psalms you will find an intimate thanksgiving for all that befalls you. In the psalms you confess your weakness and misery and thereby call down God's mercy upon you. You will find every virtue in the psalms if you are worthy of God's mercy in deigning to reveal to you their secrets.[119]

For Alcuin, as for Cassian and Bede, the psalms were not an end in themselves, but a preparation for receiving the word of God which is beyond human emotions and needs:

When the voice of psalmody acts through the intention of the heart, then a way to the heart is prepared for Almighty God, so that He may fill the innermost mind with the mysteries of prophecy or with the grace of compunction, as it is written, 'Whoso offers me praise, he honoureth me; and I will show him the way of salvation of God'. So in the sacrifice of divine praise we are shown the way to Jesus, because when through the psalms the heart is filled with compunction, a way is made by which we come to Jesus. Certainly it is appropriate that when all things are recollected in the mind it cleanses itself and breathes praise of God in the spirit, so that the heavens may be revealed to it.[120]

The psalter was for him also a summary of the revelation and prophecy contained in the rest of Scripture; it was the whole Bible compressed into one text, a *vade-mecum* for the Christian for the whole journey of life:

In the psalter to the end of your life you have material for reading, scrutinising and teaching; in it you find the prophets, the evangelists, the apostles and all the divine books spiritually

119 Alcuin, *De Psalmorum Usu Liber*, Preface, PL 101., col. 465.
120 Ibid., col. 465.

and intellectually treated and described; and the first and second coming of the Lord in prophecy. You will find both the incarnation and the passion; the resurrection and ascension of the Lord, and all the power of the divine words, in the psalms if you peruse them with the intent of the mind, and you will come by the grace of God to the marrow of intellectual understanding.[121]

Alcuin sent a little book to Bishop Arno of Salzburg by the hand of Fredegius, to encourage him in more serious and sustained devotion, and included in it the abbreviated psalter of Bede, thus introducing it with earnest recommendation into the vigorous world of the Carolingians:

> For love of you I have arranged to send through my son
> Fredegius, a little book, containing much about divine matters,
> that is: short explanations of the seven penitential psalms, also
> of psalm 119, likewise of the fifteen gradual psalms. There is also
> in this little book a small psalter which is said to be the psalter
> of the blessed priest Bede in which he collected sweet verses in
> praise of God, with prayers from each of the psalms according
> to the true Hebrew version.[122]

Where Bede had provided, and Alcuin recommended, a selection from the psalms which preserved the shape of the psalm but made it available for personal prayer, a Carolingian writer, copying the form, created a different and even more popular abbreviated psalter. Where Bede had begun from the psalter text, the new compiler began from the needs of the individual for prayers on two themes only. Taking the great themes of compunction, repentance, and thanksgiving, he selected only those verses from the psalter that expressed those ideas. Not every

121 Ibid., "Ninth Use of the Psalms," col. 467.
122 Alcuin, Letter to Arno, PL C., col. 407.

psalm, therefore, was represented, and the verses were no longer a key to the full version of the psalm. Moreover, where Bede had used the Hebrew text, he used, he says, a translation better known in his day, which Sigebert of Gembloux later suggested was the Gallican psalter.[123] The changes were deliberate, for the writer, wrongly supposed to have been Einhard, knew Bede's psalter and chose to alter it in these ways:

> The book of the psalms, although the whole of it is sacred and much better suited than the other books of holy scripture for the celebration of the Divine Office, yet all of it is not convenient for someone who wants to call upon God and beg mercy for his sins. I have therefore taken out those portions which seem appropriate for this purpose, and I have been careful to bring together a little book from them, in which if anything is found to be missing, which is thought to agree with the prayers which have been made, let it be known that what is missing is because it seems to be appropriate not for any of the members of holy church but rather for its head, which is Christ.
>
> Bede the priest of the English made these extracts before me, which would have sufficed for those who want it if it had not been made from that psalter which we call the Hebrew. But because that translation is not used in modern times I did not think it superfluous if I made one from that which at the present time the church sings to Christ over almost all the world.
>
> He who wishes to read this book, must say this three times before he begins, "O God make speed to save me; O Lord, make haste to help me". Then he should add "Glory be to the Father

---

123 Sigebert of Gembloux: "Einhard wrote a life of the Emperor Charles. . . . Imitating Bede who abbreviated the Hebrew psalter, taking out of it all the words that have to do with prayer, he (E) likewise abbreviated the Gallican psalter which we use in Gaul, taking out from it all the verses containing words of prayer." *Liber de Scriptoribus Ecclesiasticis*, PL 160, col. 566.

and to the Son and to the Holy Spirit, as it was in the beginning, is now and ever shall be, world without end, amen". Then he can begin to read, "Lord, how are they increased that trouble me" etc, to the end.[124]

It is a strange irony that Bede's extracts, which offered a way into the whole psalter, should have been supplanted by an imitator who used the selections for a more subjective purpose. Perhaps changing the text for the one well known through public worship was what determined its popularity. The change to the use of only those phrases which expressed emotion was to be even more far-reaching. Men of a solitary habit of prayer continued to make their own extracts along these lines, and increasingly the starting point was not the given words of David, but the personal need and desires of the one praying. The hermit St. Anschaire (865), for instance, did so:

> from the passages of the Bible which led to compunction he made for himself out of each psalm a little prayer . . . he was hardly concerned at all with the order of the words, he sought only compunction of heart.[125]

Whatever the changes in content, the method of abbreviation was introduced by Bede and it remained continually in use. A typical instance of its value is found in the account by Reginald of Durham of another Northern saint, the unlettered hermit Godric of Finchale, a man of much crying and tears. When he first decided to leave his flourishing trade for a life of austerity and prayer, he lived in the wooded country near Carlisle, and there someone taught him

---

124 *Testimonia Orationis Christianae Antiquioris,* ed. P. Salmon, C. Coeburgh, P. de Puncit, Corpus Christianorum Continuatio Medievalis XLVII (Turnhout, 1977), "Psalterium Abbreviatum Vercellense," ed. P. Salmon, pp. 55–78. I am greatly indebted to P. Salmon's excellent discussion and presentation of this text, pp. 36–53.

125 Ibid. p. 52, n. 2, St. Rembert's *Life of St Anschaire,* PL 118, col. 1000.

what Reginald calls "the psalter of St Jerome"[126]—abbreviations of the psalms which were in fact in the tradition of Bede. Godric, he says, was delighted with it and learned it most carefully by heart. He used this abbreviated psalter for meditation, even when he had learned to read a little by going to school with the children at the church of St. Mary in the South Bailly. In his account of this further stage of education, Reginald used words familiar in the tradition of compunction: Godric, he says, learned to listen, read, and chant, learning, meditating, and ruminating on the psalms. "Rumination," the metaphor taken from a cow chewing cud, gives a sense of eating the text, absorbing it physically, of so placing it in the memory that it becomes part of the physical person, which is how Bede's psalter was meant to be used. Reginald described Godric sitting on the step of the altar in his oratory at Finchale, holding the psalter *in gremio*, when he saw the Christ Child come out of the mouth of the figure of Christ on the cross and enter into the womb of the Virgin Mary,[127] a startlingly un-theological vision, perhaps, but one which might well have arisen out of prolonged meditation through the psalms on the double *kenosis* of Christ, who "humbled himself" by taking flesh, as well as by dying on the cross.

The tradition of the abbreviated psalter began with Bede as a memory-device, a reminder of the whole psalm, and also so that by the selected verses the heart could pray and direct itself to God in a way contained within the Scriptures. The abbreviated psalter was ideally suited to provide a structure for prayer for less learned but solitary persons, concerned only with the prayer of the heart, and it proved so for other hermits before and after Godric. But it did not remain the possession of the few. A note added to a Durham copy of the

---

126 Reginald of Durham, *Libellus de Vita et Miraculis S. Godrici, Heremitae de Finchale*, ed. J. Stevenson (London: Surtees Society, 1844), cap. IX, p. 42, cap. XVI, pp. 58–60.
127 Ibid., cap. XLI, pp. 99–101.

abbreviated psalter suggests that it should be used not only by hermits but also by laymen who

> have worldly business, who lie in sickness, who undertake long journeys, sail in ships or go to war; they sing this psalter assiduously and they gain thereby the heavenly kingdom.[128]

The abbreviated psalter contained within it the basis for the prayer of the heart for the Middle Ages, outside as well as inside the monasteries. It had a central place in the articulation of devotion, until a new age found another channel for that same compunction of heart in lengthy meditations which provided other words for the same prayer. This personal and interior prayer was a strong element in a great tradition. When in the eleventh century another man renowned for piety, a monk of Bec called Anselm, was asked to provide such "flowers from the psalms" for a great and devout lady, he sent her something more. What caught and held the interest of the eleventh century was not Anselm's selection from the psalms, which were quickly dropped, but those majestic prayers and meditations which gave a new form to the prayer of compunction and tears.[129]

At the beginning of his life, Bede learned the psalms in their Christian context; throughout his life the psalms formed him in choir, in his studies, and in his cell. At the end of his life it was the psalter which occupied him. He lived the words in which Alcuin expressed his own wondering love of the psalms:

> As angels live in heaven, so live men on earth who rejoice in the praises of God, in the pure heart of psalmody. No mortal

---

128   Ibid., quoted in p. 42, n. 1.
129   *Prayers and Meditations of St Anselm of Canterbury*, trans. with introduction Benedicta Ward SLG, (Harmondsworth, 1979). See also the penetrating discussion by R.W. Southern in *Anselm of Canterbury: A Portrait in a Landscape* (Cambridge, 1990), pp. 91–112.

man can fully declare the virtue of the psalms. In them are the confession of sins, the tears of the penitent, sorrow of heart. Here is foretold all the dispensations of our redemption, the wondrous delights of heaven's mirth. Here shall you find the Incarnation, Resurrection, and Ascension of the Word of God.[130]

130 Alcuin, Epistles IV, 391, PL C, col. 497–98.

APPENDIX
The Abbreviated Psalter of the Venerable Bede

Translated from the text edited by J. Fraipont, *Collectio Psalterii Bedae,* Corpus Christianorum Series Latina CXXII (Turnhout, 1955), pp. 452–70. The translation is based on Coverdale, Book of Common Prayer, where possible; the psalms and verses are numbered according to Bede's Vulgate psalter with the numbers of the Coverdale version following where they differ.

Psalm 1

1 Blessed is the man that hath not walked in the counsel of the ungodly and hath not sat in the seat of the scornful.

2 But his delight is in the law of the Lord and in his law will he exercise himself day and night.

3 And he shall be like a tree planted by the waterside that will bring forth his fruit in due season.

4 His leaf also shall not wither and look, whatsoever he doeth it shall prosper.

Psalm 2

10 Be wise now therefore, O ye kings, be learned, ye that are the judges of the earth.

11 Serve the Lord in fear and rejoice unto him with reverence.

12 Kiss the Son, lest he be angry and so ye perish from the right way.

Psalm 3

4/3 But thou, O Lord, art my defender, thou art my glory and the lifter up of my head.

7 Up, Lord, and help me, O my God.

Psalm 4

2/1b Have mercy upon me, and hearken unto my prayer.

Psalm 5

2/1 Ponder my words, O Lord, consider my meditation.

3/2 O hearken thou unto the voice of my calling, my King and my God, for unto thee will I make my prayer.

Psalm 6

2/1   O Lord, rebuke me not in thine indignation, neither chasten me in thy displeasure.

3/2   Have mercy upon me for I am weak; O Lord, heal me, for my bones are vexed.

4/3   My soul also is sore troubled; but Lord, how long wilt thou punish me?

5/4   Turn thee, O Lord, and deliver my soul, O save me for thy mercy's sake.

Psalm 7

2/1   O Lord my God, in thee have I put my trust, save me from all them that persecute me and deliver me.

3/2   Lest he devour my soul like a lion and tear it in pieces, while there is none to help.

Psalm 8

2/1   O Lord our Governor, how excellent is thy name in all the earth.

Psalm 9

1/2   I will be glad and rejoice in thee, yea, my songs will I make of thy name, O thou most highest.

[(Ps.10:13) Arise, O Lord, and lift up thine hand: forget not the poor.]

Psalm 10/11

6/5   His eyes consider the poor.

Psalm 11/12

3/2   Help me, O Lord.

Psalm 12/13

3/2b   How long shall mine enemies triumph over me?

4/3   Consider and hear me, O Lord my God, lighten mine eyes, that I sleep not in death.

5/4   Lest mine enemy say, I have prevailed against him.

Psalm 13/14

7/11   Then shall Jacob rejoice, and Israel shall be right glad.

Psalm 14/15

4   God maketh much of them that fear the Lord.

Psalm 15/16

1   Preserve me, O God, for in thee have I put my trust.

2   O my soul, thou said unto the Lord, thou art my God, my goods are nothing unto thee.

Psalm 16/17

    1 Consider my complaint and hearken unto my prayer.

    5 O hold thou up my goings in thy paths that my footsteps slip not.

    6 Incline thine ear unto me and hearken unto my words.

    7 Show thy marvellous loving kindness, thou that art the Saviour of them that put their trust in thee.

    8 Keep me as the apple of an eye, hide me under the shadow of thy wings.

  16 But as for me I will behold thy presence in righteousness.

Psalm 17/18

  2/1 I will love thee, O Lord, my strength.

Psalm 18/19

13/12 O cleanse thou me from my secret faults.

14/13 Keep thy servant also from presumptuous sins.

15/14 Let the words of my mouth be always acceptable in thy sight.

16/15 O Lord, my strength and my redeemer.

Psalm 19/20

  8/7 But we will remember the name of the Lord our God.

Psalm 20/21

14/13 Be thou exalted, O Lord, in thine own strength, so will we sing and praise thy power.

Psalm 21/22

20/19 Be not thou far from me, O Lord, Thou art my succour, haste thee to help me.

21/20 Deliver my soul from the sword.

22/21 Save me from the lion's mouth.

Psalm 22/23

    6 Surely thy loving-kindness and mercy shall follow me all the days of my life.

Psalm 23/24

    5 And I shall receive the blessing from the Lord.

Psalm 24/25

    1 Unto thee, O Lord, will I lift up my soul.

  4/3   Shew me thy ways, O Lord, and teach me thy truth.

  5/4 Lead me forth in thy truth and learn me, for thou art the God of my salvation.

  7/6 O remember not the sins and offences of my youth, but according to thy mercy think thou upon me.

11/10   For thy name's sake, O Lord, be merciful unto my sin for it is great.

16/15   Turn thee unto me and have mercy upon me.

17/16   O bring thou me out of my troubles.

18/17   Look upon my adversary and misery and forgive me all my sin.

20/19   O keep my soul and deliver me.

Psalm 25/26

   8   Lord, I have loved the habitation of thy house.

   9   O shut not up my soul with the sinners.

   11   O deliver me and be merciful unto me.

Psalm 26/27

   1   The Lord is my light and my salvation, whom then shall I fear?

   7/8   Hearken unto my voice, O Lord, when I cry unto thee, have mercy upon me and hear me.

   9/10   O hide not thou thy face from me, nor cast thy servant away in displeasure.

   9/11   Thou hast been my succour, leave me not, neither forsake me, O God of my salvation.

   11/13   Teach me thy way, O Lord, and lead me in the right way because of mine enemies.

   12/14   Deliver me not over into the will of mine adversaries.

   13/15   I believe verily to see the goodness of the Lord in the land of the living.

Psalm 27/28

   2   Hear the voice of my humble petitions when I cry unto thee.

   3   Do not pluck me away with the ungodly and wicked doers.

   7/8   The Lord is my strength and my shield.

Psalm 28/29

   2   O worship the Lord with holy worship.

Psalm 29/30

   11   Hear, O Lord, and have mercy upon me, Lord, be thou my helper.

   13   So that I may sing of thy praise and not be silent, O Lord God, I will give thanks to thee forever.

Psalm 30/31

   2/1   In thee, O Lord, have I put my trust, let me never be put to confusion, deliver me in thy righteousness.

   3/2   Bow down thine ear to me, make haste to deliver me.

   4/4; 6   For thou art my strong rock and house of defence, into thy hands I commend my spirit.

16/17   My time is in thine hand, deliver me from the hand of mine enemies and from them that persecute me.

17/18   Shew thy servant the light of thy countenance, and save me for thy mercy's sake.

Psalm 31/32

1   Blessed is he whose unrighteousness is forgiven and whose sin is covered.

5   I will acknowledge my sin unto thee and mine un-righteousness have I not hid.

7/8   Thou art a place to hide me in, thou shalt preserve me from trouble.

Psalm 32/33

18/17   Behold the eye of the Lord is upon them that fear him and upon them that put their trust in his mercy.

Psalm 33/34

2/1   I will always give thanks unto the Lord, his praise shall ever be in my mouth.

4/3   O praise the Lord with me and let us magnify his name together.

5/4   I sought the Lord and he heard me, yea, he delivered me out of all my fear.

9/8   O taste and see how gracious the Lord is; blessed is the man that trusteth in him.

10/9   O fear the Lord, ye that are his saints, for they that fear him lack nothing.

11b/10b They who seek the Lord shall want no manner of thing that is good.

21/20   The Lord keepeth all his bones, so that not one of them shall be broken.

23/22   The Lord delivereth the souls of his servants.

Psalm 34/35

1   Plead thou my cause, O Lord, with them that strive with me, and fight thou against them that fight against me.

2   Lay hand upon shield and buckler and stand up to help me.

3b   Say unto my soul, I am thy salvation.

9   And my soul, be joyful in the Lord, it shall rejoice in his salvation.

18   I will give thee thanks in the great congregation.

28   And as for my tongue it shall be talking of thy righteousness and of thy praise all the day long.

Psalm 35/36

6/5 Thy mercy, O Lord, reacheth unto the heavens.

8/7b How excellent is thy mercy, O God.

10/9 For with thee is the well of life, and in thy light shall we see light.

11/10 O continue forth thy loving kindness unto them that know thee, and thy righteousness unto them that are true of heart.

12/11 O let not the foot of pride come against me, and let not the hand of the ungodly cast me down.

Psalm 36/37

25 I have been young, and now am old, and yet I never saw the righteous forsaken.

28 For the Lord loves the thing that is right, he forsaketh not his that be godly, but they are preserved forever.

40 The Lord shall stand by them.

Psalm 37/38

2/1 Put me not to rebuke, O Lord, in thine anger, neither chasten me in thy heavy displeasure.

16/15 For in thee, O Lord, have I put my trust, thou shalt answer for me, O Lord my God.

22/21 Forsake me not, O Lord my God, be not thou far from me.

22/23 Haste thee to help me, O Lord God of my salvation.

Psalm 38/39

8b Truly my hope is even in thee.

9 Deliver me from all mine offences, and make me not a rebuke unto the foolish.

11 Take thy plague away from me.

Psalm 39/40

2/1 I waited patiently for the Lord and he inclined unto me and heard my calling.

14/16 Make haste, O Lord, to help me.

17/19 Let those that seek thee be joyful and glad in thee.

18/21 Thou art my helper and redeemer, make no long tarrying, O my God.

Psalm 40/41

5/4 I said, Lord be merciful unto me, heal my soul, for I have sinned against thee.

11/10 But be thou merciful unto me, O Lord.

Psalm 41/42

2/1   Like as the hart desireth the waterbrooks, so longeth my soul after thee, O God.

Psalm 42/43

1   Give sentence with me, O God, and defend my cause against the ungodly people; O deliver me from the deceitful and wicked man.

2   For thou art the God of my strength, why hast thou put me from thee?

Psalm 43/44

26   Arise and help us and deliver us for thy mercy's sake.

Psalm 44/45

18b   Thy seat, O God, endureth for ever, the sceptre of thy kingdom is a right sceptre, therefore shall the people give thanks unto thee world without end.

Psalm 45/46

1   God is our hope and strength, a very present help in trouble.

Psalm 46/47

3/2b   He is the great king upon all the earth:

7/6   O sing praises, sing praises unto our God, O sing praises, sing praises unto our King!

Psalm 47/48

15/13   For this God is our God forever and ever, he shall be our guide unto death.

Psalm 48/49

16/15   Truly God hath redeemeth my soul from the place of hell, for he shall receive me.

Psalm 49/50

1   The Lord, even the most mighty God, hath spoken.

8   I will not reprove thee because of thy sacrifices or for thy burnt offerings, because they were not always before me.

9   I will take no bullock out of thine house nor he-goat out of thy folds.

10   For all the beasts of the forest are mine.

11   I know all the fowls upon the mountains and the wild beasts of the field are in my sight.

12   If I be hungry, I will not tell thee, for the whole world is mine and all that is therein.

14   Offer unto God thanksgiving and pay thy vows unto the most highest.

15   And call upon me in the time of trouble, I will set thee free and thou shalt praise me.

23/22 Whoso offereth me thanks and praise, he honoureth me and to him that ordereth his conversation right will I shew the salvation of God.

Psalm 50/51

3/1 Have mercy upon me, O God, after thy great goodness, according to the multitude of thy mercies do away mine offences.

4/2 Wash me thoroughly from my wickedness and cleanse me from my sins.

5/3 For I acknowledge my faults and my sin is ever before me.

6/4 Against thee only have I sinned and done this evil in thy sight.

11/9 Turn thy face from my sins and put out all my misdeeds; make me a clean heart, O God, and renew a right spirit within me.

13/11 Cast me not away from thy presence and take not thy Holy Spirit from me.

14/12 Restore to me the joy of thy salvation and strengthen me with thy free spirit.

16/14 Deliver me from blood-guiltiness, O God, for thou art the God of my salvation and my tongue shall sing of thy righteousness.

17/15 Thou shalt open my lips, O Lord, and my mouth shall shew thy praise.

19/17 The sacrifice of God is a troubled spirit, a broken and contrite heart, O God, shalt thou not despise.

Psalm 51/52

3/2 The goodness of God endureth yet daily.

Psalm 52/53

7/8 Then should Jacob rejoice and Israel should be right glad.

Psalm 53/54

3/1 Save me, O God, for thy name's sake and avenge me in thy strength.

4/2 Hear my prayer, O God, and hearken unto the words of my mouth.

Psalm 54/55

2/1 Hear my prayer, O God, and hide not thyself from my petition;

3/2a take heed unto me and hear me.

Psalm 55/56

4/3 Though I am sometime afraid, yet put I my trust in Thee.

5/4b I have put my trust in God and will not fear what flesh can do unto me.

Psalm 56/57

2/1 Be merciful unto me, O God, be merciful unto me, for my soul trusteth in thee; under the shadow of thy wings shall be my refuge until this tyranny be overpast;

3/2   I will call upon the most high God, even unto the God which shall perform the cause which I have in hand.

4/3a He shall send from heaven and save me.

Psalm 57/58

12/10 Verily there is a God that judgeth the earth.

Psalm 58/59

2/1   Deliver me from mine enemies, O God, defend me from them that rise up against me.

10/9 My strength will I ascribe unto thee for thou art the God of my refuge.

11/10a God sheweth me his goodness plenteously,

17/16b for thou hast been my defence and refuge in the day of my trouble.

18/17 Unto thee, O my strength, will I sing, for thou, O God, art my refuge and my merciful God.

Psalm 59/60

13/11 O be thou our help in trouble, for vain is the help of man.

14/12 Through God will we do great acts, for it is he that shall tread down our enemies.

Psalm 60/61

2/1   Hear my crying, O Lord, give ear unto my prayer:

3/4   from the ends of the earth will I call upon thee when my heart is in heaviness. O set me up upon a rock that is higher than I,

4/5   for thou hast been my hope and a strong tower for me against mine enemy.

5/4   I will dwell in thy tabernacle for ever and my trust shall be under the covering of thy wings.

6/5   For thou, Lord, hast heard my desires and hast given an heritage unto those that fear thy name;

8/7   O prepare thy loving mercy and faithfulness.

Psalm 61/62

6/5   In him is my hope,

7/6   he truly is my strength and my salvation, he is my defence so that I shall not fall.

Psalm 62/63

2/1   O God, thou art my God, early will I seek thee, my soul thirsteth for thee, my flesh longeth after thee;

3   thus have I looked for thee in holiness, that I might behold thy power and glory;

4 for thy loving-kindness is better than life itself; my lips shall praise thee.

5 As long as I live will I magnify thee and lift up my hands in thy name,

8 because thou hast been my helper, therefore under the shadow of thy wings will I rejoice.

Psalm 63/64

2/1 Hear my voice, O God, in my prayer, preserve my life from fear of the enemy.

Psalm 64/65

6/5 Hear us, O God of our salvation.

Psalm 65/66

4/3 All the world shall worship thee, sing of thee and praise thy name.

8/7 O praise our God, ye people, and make the voice of his praise to be heard,

9/8a who holdeth our soul in life.

20/18 Praised be God, who hath not cast out my prayer nor turned his mercy from me.

Psalm 66/67

2/1 God be merciful unto us and bless us and shew us the light of his countenance.

7/6 God, even our own God, shall give us his blessing.

8 God shall bless us.

Psalm 67/68

2/1 Let God arise and let his enemies be scattered, let them also that hate him flee before him;

4/3 but let the righteous be glad and rejoice before God, let them also be merry and joyful.

Psalm 68/69

17 Hear me, O Lord, for thy loving kindness is comfortable, turn thee unto me according to the multitude of thy mercies,

18 and hide not thy face from thy servant for I am in trouble, O haste thee and hear me.

19 Draw nigh unto my soul and save it, O deliver me, because of mine enemies.

30 Thy help, O God, shall lift me up.

Psalm 69/70

2/1 Haste thee, O God, to deliver me, make haste to help me, O Lord.

5/4a Let all those that seek thee be joyful and glad in thee.

6/5–6 As for me, I am poor and in misery, haste thee unto me, O God; thou art my helper and redeemer, O Lord, make no long tarrying.

Psalm 70/71

1 In thee, O Lord, have I put my trust, let me never be put to confusion,

2 but rid me and deliver me in thy righteousness, incline thine ear unto me and save me.

4/3–4 Deliver me, O my God, out of the hand of the ungodly, out of the hand of the unrighteous and cruel man,

5/4a for thou, O Lord God, art the thing that I long for;

10/12 go not far from me, O God. My God, haste thee to help me.

Psalm 71/72

17 Thy name shall endure for ever, thy name shall remain under the sun.

Psalm 72/73

28/27 But it is good for me to hold me fast by God, to put my trust in the Lord God.

Psalm 73/74

12/13 For God is my King of old.

19/20 O deliver not the soul of thy turtle-dove unto the multitude of the enemies, and forget not the congregation of the poor for ever.

Psalm 74/75

10/11 But I will talk of the God of Jacob and praise him for ever.

Psalm 75/76

10/9 When God arose to judgement and to help all the meek upon earth.

Psalm 76/77

2/1 I will cry unto God with my voice, even unto God will I cry with my voice and he shall hearken unto me.

3/2a In the time of my trouble I sought the Lord.

Psalm 77/78

38 But he was so merciful that he forgave their misdeeds and destroyed them not.

Psalm 78/79

8 O remember not our old sins but have mercy upon us and that soon, for we are come to great misery.

9 Help us, O God our Jesus, for the glory of thy name, O deliver us and be merciful unto our sins for thy name's sake.

Psalm 79/80

3/2b Stir up thy strength and come and help us.

8/7 Turn us again, thou God of hosts, shew the light of thy countenance and we shall be whole.

Psalm 80/81

2/1 Sing we merrily unto God our strength.

Psalm 81/82

3 Defend the poor and fatherless, see that such as are in need and necessity have right.

4 Deliver the outcast and poor, save them from the hand of the ungodly.

Psalm 82/83

2/1 Hold not thy tongue, O God, keep not still silence,

19/18 and they shall know that thou whose name is our God art only the most highest over all the earth.

Psalm 83/84

9/8 O Lord God of hosts, hear my prayer,

13 O Lord of hosts, blessed is the man that putteth his trust in thee.

Psalm 84/85

5/4 Turn us then, O God our Saviour, and let thine anger cease from us.

6/5 Be not displeased with us forever.

8/7 Shew us thy mercy, O Lord, and grant us thy salvation.

Psalm 85/86

1 Bow down thine ear, O Lord, and hear me, for I am poor and in misery.

3-4 Be merciful unto me, O Lord, for I will call daily upon thee, comfort the soul of thy servant, for unto thee, O Lord, do I lift up my soul.

5 For thou, Lord, art good and gracious, and of great mercy unto all them that call upon thee.

6 Give ear, Lord, unto my prayer and ponder the voice of my humble desires.

7 In the time of my trouble I will call upon thee, for thou hearest me.

11 Teach me thy way, O Lord, and I will walk in thy truth, O knit my heart unto thee that I may fear thy name.

12 I will thank thee, O Lord, with all my heart, and will praise thy name for evermore.

15-16 But thou, O Lord, art full of compassion and mercy, O turn thee then unto me and have mercy upon me, give thy strength unto thy servant and help the son of thy handmaid.

17 Shew some token upon me for good that they who hate me may see it and be ashamed, because thou, Lord, hast holpen me and comforted me.

Psalm 86/87

7 The singers also and the trumpeters shall he rehearse; all my fresh springs shall be in thee.

Psalm 87/88

3/1b O let my prayer enter into thy presence, incline thine ear unto my calling.

14/13 Unto thee have I cried, O Lord, and early shall my prayer come before thee.

Psalm 88/89

6/5 O Lord, the very heavens shall praise thy works.

15b Mercy and truth shall go before thy face.

Psalm 89/90

16 Shew thy servants thy work and thy children thy glory,

17 and the glorious majesty of the Lord our God be upon us, prosper thou the work of our hands upon us, O prosper thou our handiwork.

Psalm 90/91

9 For thou, Lord, art my hope.

Psalm 91/92

5/4 For thou, Lord, hast made me glad through thy works.

Psalm 92/93

5 Thy testimonies, O Lord, are very sure.

Psalm 93/94

18 Thy mercy, O Lord, held me up.

Psalm 94/95

6–7 O come, let us worship and fall down, and kneel before the Lord our Maker, for he is the Lord our God.

Psalm 95/96

6 Glory and worship are before him.

Psalm 96/97

10 O ye that love the Lord see that ye hate the thing that is evil, the Lord preserveth the souls of his saints, he shall deliver them from the hand of the ungodly.

Psalm 97/98

3–4 He hath remembered his mercy.

Psalm 98/99

　　5　O magnify the Lord our God.

Psalm 99/100

　2/1b　Serve the Lord with gladness and come before his presence with a song.

　3/2　Be ye sure that the Lord, he is God, it is he that hath made us, we are his people.

Psalm 100/101

　　1　My song shall be of mercy and judgement.

　　3　I will sing and when thou wilt come unto me I will walk in my house with a perfect heart.

Psalm 101/102

　2/1　Hear my prayer, O Lord, and let my crying come unto thee, hide not thy face from me in the time of my trouble.

　3/2　O hear me and that right soon.

Psalm 102/103

　　1　Praise the Lord, O my soul, and all that is within me praise his holy name.

　　2　Praise the Lord, O my soul, and forget not all his benefits.

　　3　Who forgiveth all thy sin, and healeth all thine infirmities.

　　4　Who saveth thy life from destruction and crowneth thee with mercy and loving-kindness.

Psalm 103/104

　　1　Praise the Lord, O my soul, O Lord my God, thou art becoming exceeding glorious, thou art clothed with majesty and honour.

　31　The glorious majesty of the Lord shall endure forever, the Lord shall rejoice in all his works.

Psalm 104/105

　　4　Seek the Lord and his strength, seek his face evermore.

　　5　Remember the marvellous works that he hath done.

Psalm 106/107

　　1　O give thanks unto the Lord for he is gracious and his mercy endureth forever.

　　8　O that men would therefore praise the Lord for his goodness and declare the wonders that he doeth for the children of men.

　　9　For he satisfieth the empty soul and filleth the hungry soul with goodness.

Psalm 107/108

13/12   O help us against the enemy, for vain is the help of man.

14/13   Through God we shall do great acts and it is he that shall tread down our enemies.

Psalm 108/109

21/20   But deal thou with me, O Lord God, according to thy Name, for sweet is thy mercy; O deliver me, for I am helpless and poor.

26/25   Help me, O Lord my God, O save me according to thy mercy.

Psalm 109/110

2   Be thou ruler even in the midst among thine enemies.

Psalm 110/111

1   I will give thanks unto the Lord with my whole heart.

3   His work is worthy to be praised and had in honour.

7   The works of his hands are verity and judgement.

Psalm 111/112

1   Blessed is the man that feareth the Lord, he hath great delight in his commandments.

7   The righteous shall be had in everlasting remembrance, he will not be afraid of any evil tidings.

Psalm 112/113

2   Blessed be the name of the Lord from this time forth for evermore.

Psalm 113/115

9/1   Not unto us, O Lord, not unto us, but unto thy name give the praise, for thy loving mercy and for thy truth's sake.

Psalm 114/116

4   O Lord, I beseech thee, deliver my soul.

Psalm 115/116

4/12   I will call upon the name of the Lord.

6/13   Right dear in the sight of the Lord is the death of his saints.

Psalm 116/117

2   And the truth of the Lord endureth for ever.

Psalm 117/118

6   The Lord is on my side, I will not fear what man doeth unto me.

7   The Lord taketh my part with them that help me, therefore shall I see my desire upon mine enemies.

9/8   It is better to trust in the Lord than to put any confidence in man.

21   I will thank thee, Lord, for thou hast heard me, and art become my salvation.

Psalm 118/119

7   I will thank thee with an unfeigned heart when I shall have learned the judgements of thy righteousness.

10   O let me not go wrong out of thy commandments.

18   Open thou mine eyes that I may see the wondrous things of thy law.

29   Take from me the way of lying and cause thou me to make much of thy law.

36   Incline mine heart unto thy testimonies and not to covetousness.

41   Let thy loving mercy come also unto me, O Lord, even thy salvation according unto thy word.

50   The same is my comfort in my trouble for thy word hath quickened me.

64   The earth, O Lord, is full of thy mercy, O teach me thy statutes.

67   Before I was troubled I went wrong.

68   Thou art good and gracious, O teach me thy statutes.

76   O let thy merciful kindness be my comfort according to thy word unto thy servant.

88   O quicken me after thy loving-kindness and so shall I keep the testimonies of thy mouth.

92   If my delight had not been in thy law, I should have perished in my trouble.

103   O how sweet are thy words unto my throat, yea, sweeter than honey unto my mouth.

108   Let the freewill offerings of my mouth please thee, O Lord, and teach me thy judgements.

116   O stablish me according to thy word that I may live.

117   Hold thou me up and I shall be safe.

124   O deal with thy servant according to thy loving mercy and teach me thy statutes.

132   O look thou upon me and be merciful unto me,

135   and teach me thy statutes.

137   Righteous art thou, O Lord, and true is thy judgement.

149   Hear my voice, O Lord, according unto thy loving-kindness, quicken me, according as thou art wont.

153   O consider mine adversity and deliver me.

159   O quicken me according to thy loving-kindness.

165   Great is the peace that they have who love thy law and they are not offended at it.

169 Let my praise come before thee, O Lord, give me understanding according to thy word.

170 Let my supplication come before thee, deliver me, according to thy word.

Psalm 119/120

2/1 Deliver my soul, O Lord, from lying lips, and from a deceitful tongue.

Psalm 120/121

1 I will lift up mine eyes unto the hills, from whence cometh my help?

Psalm 121/122

6 They shall prosper that love thee.

Psalm 122/123

3 Have mercy upon us, O Lord, have mercy upon us.

Psalm 123/124

8/7 Our help is in the name of the Lord, who hath made heaven and earth.

Psalm 124/125

4 Do well, O Lord, unto those that are good and true of heart.

Psalm 125/126

4/5 Turn our captivity, O Lord, as the rivers in the south.

Psalm 126/127

1/2 Except the Lord keep the city the watchman waketh but in vain.

Psalm 127/128

1 Blessed are they that fear the Lord and walk in his ways.

Psalm 128/129

8 The Lord prosper you.

Psalm 129/130

1–2 Lord, hear my voice, O let thine ears consider well the voice of my complaint.

Psalm 130/131

1 Lord, I am not high-minded, I have no proud looks.

Psalm 131/132

14/15 This shall be my rest for ever.

Psalm 132/133

3/4 For there the Lord promised his blessing and life for evermore.

Psalm 133/134

1 Ye who stand in the house of the Lord.

Psalm 134/135

3 O praise the Lord, for the Lord is gracious.

Psalm 135/136

26 O give thanks unto the God of heaven, for his mercy endureth for ever.

[Ps. 136? Blessed is the man who loves the Lord.[131]]

Psalm 137/138

1 I will give thanks unto thee, O Lord, with my whole heart.

8 Thy mercy, O Lord, endureth for ever, despise not then the works of thine own hands.

Psalm 138/139

8/7 If I climb up into heaven thou art there; if I go down into hell thou art there also.

Psalm 139/140

1 Deliver me, O Lord, from the evil man and preserve me from the wicked man.

Psalm 140/141

1 Consider my voice when I cry unto thee.

2 Let my prayer be set forth in thy sight as the incense.

3 Set a watch, O Lord, before my mouth and keep the door of my lips.

Psalm 141/142

8/9 O bring my soul out of prison that I may give thanks unto thy name.

Psalm 142/143

1 Hear my prayer, O Lord, hearken unto me for thy righteousness sake;

2 and enter not into judgement with thy servant for in thy sight shall no man living be justified.

8 O let me hear of thy loving-kindness betimes in the morning, for in thee is my trust; shew thou me the way that I should walk in for I lift up my soul unto thee.

9 Deliver me, O Lord, from mine enemies, for I flee unto thee to hide me;

10 Teach me to do the thing that pleaseth thee, for thou art my God; let thy loving spirit lead me forth into the land of righteousness.

11 Quicken me, O Lord, for thy name's sake and for thy righteousness' sake,

12 for I am thy servant.

---

131 For discussion of the verse, see pages 51–52.

Psalm 143/144

1-2 Blessed be the Lord my strength, my hope and my fortress, my castle and deliverer.

Psalm 144/145

2 Every day I will give thanks unto thee and praise thy name forever and ever.

21 My mouth shall speak the praise of the Lord, and let all flesh give thanks unto his holy Name forever and ever.

Psalm 145/146

2/1 Praise the Lord, O my soul, while I live will I praise the Lord, yea, as long as I have any being I will sing praises unto my God.

Psalm 146/147

1 Praise the Lord,

11 for it is a good thing to sing praises unto our God; the Lord's delight is in them that fear him and put their trust in his mercy.

Psalm 146/47

18 He sendeth out his word and melteth them.

Psalm 148

1 O praise the Lord of heaven, praise him in the height.

2 Praise him all ye angels of his, praise him, all his host.

3 Praise him, sun and moon, praise him all ye stars and light.

4 Praise him, all ye heavens, and ye waters that are above the heavens.

11 Praise the Lord, kings of the earth and all peoples, princes and all judges of the world.

12 Young men and maidens, old men and children, praise the name of the Lord,

13/12 for his name only is excellent,

14/13 and his praise above heaven and earth; he shall exalt the horn of his people, all his saints shall praise him.

Psalm 149

1 O sing unto the Lord a new song, let the congregation of saints praise him.

4 He helpeth the meek-hearted.

5 Let the saints be joyful with glory, let them rejoice in their beds.

6 Let the praises of God be in their mouth.

Psalm 150

6 Let everything that hath breath praise the Lord.

4
A TRUE EASTER
THE SYNOD *of* WHITBY

❖ ▪ ❖ ▪ ❖ ❖ ▪ ❖ ▪ ❖ ▪ ❖ ▪ ❖ ▪ ❖

I

I
n 664 a meeting was held at Whitby to discuss the date upon which
Easter should be celebrated. Why discuss this old debate now?
Partly out of love of the northern kingdom where it happened
and of the writer who tells about it; but more than that, because the
debate about Easter at Whitby in 664 shows how easily a secular appeal
to uniformity can be confused with a theological concern for unity. In
any group, there is always more beneath the surface of topics discussed.
Those concerned with public life in church, state, and university are
rapidly made aware of hidden pitfalls and opportunities similar to those
in seventh-century Northumbria. A study of these texts shows both
how the past can be manipulated by modern debates, and also how,
in terms of their own times, quite a different conclusion about them
should be reached.

The seventh century was the golden age of Christianity in
Northumbria, and it is often suggested that its pivotal moment was in
664 at the meeting held at the abbey at Whitby to decide on the date
on which the Northumbrians would celebrate Easter. This meeting
has been presented often enough as a clash between two kinds of
Christianity, as an antagonism that was continual and deep. This has led
to the view that there was an irreconcilable difference between Irish and

Roman missionaries, finally culminating in a clash between charismatic simplicity and legal power about the date of Easter. But it was in no way an anti-Irish, pro-Roman tussle. That was the view of churchmen in the nineteenth century who were concerned with their own problems about English–Roman church differences, and not of seventh-century Northumbria.[132] It is a misconception which is now creating the fantasy of a "Celtic spirituality."[133] This "looking-glass approach" to history is an instance of how division can be created by a reading of history which explores the past in order to find present problems there, not seeing the past in its own light. Concern for the Easter date was a much wider and profounder question than nationalism, and it also involved non-church matters which brought a demand not for unity but for uniformity. It was not seen by the participants as a quarrel between different styles of Christianity, institutional Roman and free-spirited Celt; both were concerned with the same problem and went about solving it in the same way. What united them was far more profound than what divided them.

There were at least two issues discussed at Whitby, not just one. There was the situation of two differing dates for the celebration of Easter. This was not a frequent or an obvious clash, and it does not seem to have been a cause for conflict previously. According to both Bede and Eddius Stephanus, it was highlighted at that moment by external and domestic matters:

> Queen Eanflaed and her people . . . observed (Easter) as she
> had seen it done in Kent. . . . Hence it is said that in these days
> it sometimes happened that Easter was celebrated twice in the
> same year, so that the king had finished the fast and was keeping

132 Cf. Edmund Bishop, *Liturgica Historica* (Oxford, 1917), chap. 19, "About an Old Prayer Book," pp. 384–91.
133 Bookshops now stock shelves full of books on "Celtic spirituality," many of which have nothing either Celtic or spiritual about them.

Easter Sunday, while the queen and her people were still in Lent and observing Palm Sunday.[134]

The other problem was two styles of hair-cut, something immediately seen, and therefore a more noticeable difference than Easter. External signs matter in non-writing societies, and whether the shaving was of the whole head, the circle at the back only, or the front only, was something visible and obvious.[135] Bede and Ceolfrith in their letter to Nechtan noted the hair-cut problem and, while saying that it was not really vital to theology, argued their point of view as a matter of uniformity only.[136] It certainly mattered enough in England for Theodore to wait six months for his shaved hair to grow so that he could be re-tonsured before he came to take up his post as seventh archbishop of Canterbury.[137] Differences about the date of the celebration of Easter were less frequently noticed, but were theologically more important: the whole year depended on the date of Easter, with its preparatory days of Lent and the next fifty days of Pentecost, both times for baptism and the preparation for baptism. It was not possible, therefore, to wait to see each year when the full moon would be the Paschal moon; it was an astronomical problem of forecasting years ahead.

The main source for information about the Easter controversy in Northumbria is Bede's *Ecclesiastical History of the English People*. In his history of the English nation as a race new-born into Christ, Bede placed at the centre a chapter which gives an account of the discussion at the Council of Whitby in 664 of the differing dates at which Easter was celebrated by the Christians of the new Roman and the old Roman-Irish traditions.[138] In book five he also quoted at length a letter

---

134 Bede, *Ecclesiastical History of the English People*, ed. and trans. B. Colgrave and R. A. B. Mynors (Oxford, 1969) (hereafter referred to as EH), Bk. 3: 24, p. 297.
135 *Apologia de Barbis*, CCSM. This contains three medieval treatises about beards and hair-cuts.
136 EH, Bk. 5: 21, pp. 546–49.
137 EH, Bk. 4: 1, p. 331.
138 EH, Bk. 3: 25, pp. 295–309.

to Nechtan, king of the Picts, which contains a detailed explanation of the problem.[139] In the *Ecclesiastical History of the English People*, Bede told the story of a newly converted barbarian people, their history seen under the lens of the gospel, as they became part of the Church which was living in the sixth and last age of the world. His interest in them was theological, and his account of the debates at Whitby reflect this. He was also an excellent mathematician[140] and wrote elsewhere about the astronomical as well as the spiritual aspect of the matter. His sources for his account were almost certainly oral reminiscences of those who had been there, which was for him a major historical source, as he explained in his Preface.[141] One written source he may have known was Eddius Stephanus's *Life of Saint Wilfrid*,[142] a much briefer account, though substantially the same as that of Bede; after all, Bede knew and had spoken with Wilfrid, the main participant.[143] There were other people still alive who had been there as well as Wilfrid. No historian can claim to be entirely impartial, but it would be unfair to think of Bede as a blind supporter of a Roman-style tradition. In himself Bede represented Anglo-Saxon, Roman-Irish, and Gaulish-Roman traditions. He was by birth an Anglo-Saxon, and he lived from the age of seven in the monastery founded on the Roman pattern by the Anglo-Saxon thane Benedict Biscop with the significant dedication to St. Peter and St. Paul, the apostles who were celebrated as martyrs in Rome. There is in Bede's life and works a sense of wonder and

139 EH, Bk. 5: 21, pp. 533–53. The letter is attributed to Ceolfrith, but there can be no doubt about Bede's involvement with the text.
140 Bede, *De Temporibus*, in *Bedae opera didascalica*, ed. C. W. Jones, 3 vols., CCSL (Turnhout: Brepols, 1975–1980) (hereafter BOD). For extensive discussion, cf. *Bedae opera de temporibus*, ed. with introduction by C. W. Jones (Cambridge, MA: Medieval Academy of America, 1943), and *Bede: The Reckoning of Time*, trans. with introduction and commentary by Faith Wallis (Liverpool: Liverpool University Press, 1999).
141 EH, Preface, pp. 3–7.
142 Eddius Stephanus, *Life of St Wilfrid*, ed. and trans. Bertram Colgrave (Cambridge, 1927).
143 EH, Bk. 4: 19, pp. 391–93.

delight at all the riches of Christian culture brought to his race by the missionaries from Gaul and Rome, but also an equal respect for much that came to the island from Rome through Ireland. He was formed by and devoted to the Mediterranean Latin tradition of Christianity, but he saw it as being received from more than one source: from Rome through Gaul, certainly, but also from Rome through Ireland. Bede's account of the council was therefore not likely to reflect anything other than this sense of unity.

The meeting was held in the royal foundation of the Irish monk Aidan and Hilda at Whitby, on the borders between Deira and Bernicia; it became the burial place of Anglo-Saxon kings of Northumbria. The meeting was called by Bede *synodus*—that is, a meeting for consultation—but it was not necessarily a "Church council." It seems more profitable to regard it as a meeting of the king and his thanes and the local bishop to decide about many things, rather than to see it in terms of later Church councils such as Hatfield. It was called by the king; he presided, and the language of most people present was English; Cedd was employed as a translator from both Irish and Latin. As with early Church councils, such as Nicea, the difference between a Church council and a secular meeting should not be pushed too far; but this was the seventh and not the fourth century, and bishops were perfectly capable of calling their own councils for Church affairs. Here there was no archbishop present: Deusdedit of Canterbury was ill and died in July that year,[144] and there was a thirty-year vacancy at York, which in any case was not then an archbishopric. The bishops present were Cedd and Agilbert, both bishops without portfolio; there was also Colman, who was Oswy's local bishop of Lindisfarne and a monk of Iona.

When we look at who said what and why, it was all more mixed than at first appears. It was, after all, not a matter of the arrogant men

144 EH, Bk. 4: 1, p. 329.

from Rome baring their teeth at the simple Irish. At the Council of Whitby, who supported which side? There was no clear-cut division among the participants in terms of nationalism. An epitome of the mingling of traditions is seen in Hilda, the hostess on this occasion. Hilda was an Anglo-Saxon princess (614–680), younger daughter of Hereric, nephew of Edwin of Northumbria and of Breguswith. She was born while her father was a prisoner in Elmet of the British, who later killed him by poison. Before her birth, her mother, feeling a sense of great loss, dreamt that she found "a most precious necklace under her garment . . . such a blaze of light that it filled all Britain with its grace and splendour."[145]

Hilda was brought up at the court of the Anglo-Saxon Edwin. One sister, Hereswith, married the Anglo-Saxon king of East Anglia, then became a nun at the convent of Chelles in Gaul.[146] Hilda was baptised with Edwin and his court on April 12th 627, aged thirteen, in the new church dedicated to St. Peter in York by Paulinus.[147] She was almost certainly part of the group of nobles who fled south with the queen when Edwin was killed by Aethelred in 633.[148] Thus, by birth one of the Anglo-Saxons, she first experienced the Christianity brought by the Roman missionaries, a tradition emphasized by her later life in Gaul and Kent.

In 647, twenty years later, when she was thirty-three, Hilda decided to be a nun and went to her nephew in East Anglia for a year, planning to join her sister in the Gaulish convent at Chelles. But she came to know and revere the Irish missionary from Iona, Aidan, and he persuaded her to stay in England. At first she was part of a new group at Hartlepool, but then, when the abbess Heiu left for a life of greater

145 EH, Bk. 4: 23, p. 411.
146 EH, Bk. 4: 23, p. 407.
147 Ibid.
148 EH, Bk. 2: 20, p. 205.

seclusion, Hilda became abbess of Whitby.[149] Hilda was hostess to the Council of Whitby, where, though by her birth and baptism and life in exile one would have expected her to be a Romanist, because of the influence of Aidan and Colman she in fact inclined towards the Irish side. In her life there is a mixture of Anglo-Saxon, Roman, and Irish elements which blended together imperceptibly.

No clear line can be drawn about others either. Cedd, the Anglo-Saxon founder of Lastingham, was made bishop on Iona for the East Saxons and consecrated by the Irish, but he acted as a careful and impartial interpreter at Whitby. King Oswy, who called the council, was from an Anglo-Saxon royal house, had been baptised by the Irish, spoke Irish, and was a close friend of Colman, but accepted in the end without hesitation the new Roman calculation. Wilfrid himself, the architect of the Roman arguments and the first Englishman to appeal to Rome, had been educated in the Irish monastery of Lindisfarne. Agilbert, who ordained Wilfrid priest, though born in Gaul, had been educated in Ireland. Prince Aldfrith, who was a friend of Wilfrid, gave him the abbey of Ripon only after offering it to Eata of Melrose, "who followed the Irish ways."[150] The illegitimate son of an Anglo-Saxon king and an Irish princess, Aldfrith had been educated in Ireland, but supported and indeed initiated the Roman arguments at Whitby. Colman was an Irish monk of Iona appointed as bishop of Lindisfarne, but a friend of the Anglo-Saxon Oswy. James the Deacon was an Italian, a companion of Paulinus who had stayed behind in Northumbria in 633 for a year under persecution and then continued to live there in a land dominated by Iona and "instructed many in singing after the manner of Rome and the Kentish people";[151] a quiet, elderly musician, he was nevertheless a participant at Whitby with experience of all sides.

149 EH, Bk. 3: 23, pp. 404–9.
150 EH, Bk. 3: 25, p. 299.
151 EH, Bk. 2: 20, p. 207.

So almost everyone at Whitby had close and friendly contact with both Roman and Irish missionaries; it was not a clash of opposites, but an argument between friends on a matter, the importance of which united them far more than the details divided. There was no sense that Romans were good and Irish were bad. In this matter of the Easter date, what needed sorting out were errors of calculation, whoever did it. Likewise with conduct: no-one was judged as Roman, English, or Irish; such divisions were not appropriate. Roman missionaries, Anglo-Saxons, and Irish were all in their conduct as Christians praised for some things and not admired for others.

For instance, the Irish were praised for many apostolic virtues, but there were facets of the Irish character that were not seen as admirable, even when linked to evangelical zeal. They were fervent preachers, but their readiness to correct others was not always an advantage. Perhaps a certain challenge and fierceness was needed in the lands of the Irish, where there had been Christians since the days of Patrick, but the English were not yet Christian; they "needed the milk of the word." So, when a fierce hell-fire preacher was sent to Northumbria from Iona, he was sent home again and replaced by the wiser Aidan.[152] The Irish temper was not even very efficacious among themselves: when Ronan, an Irishman who had been in Gaul and accepted the new calculations for Easter, argued with his compatriot on the subject, Finan of Iona, "who was a man of fierce temper," he enraged him instead of convincing him by the way in which he disputed with him.[153] The worldly life of the Anglo-Saxon nuns at Coldingham was rebuked by the Irishman Adamnan, with whom Bede had argued in a friendly way about the form of tonsure appropriate to monks;[154] he saw fire descending on their monastery even though they had begun under the care of the royal Anglo-Saxon queen Aebba, a friend of Cuthbert.

152 EH, Bk. 3: 5, p. 229.
153 EH, Bk. 3: 25, pp. 275–77.
154 EH, Bk. 5: 22, p. 551.

There were other tensions at Whitby, however, which influenced the outcome, and these were connected with the son and daughter of Oswy. Eanflaeda, the wife of Oswy, may or may not have been present at the council, but was certainly a powerful influence on the Easter debate. Bertha, a Merovingian princess from Gaul, was her grandmother, and her mother was Aethelburgh, wife of Edwin, sister of Eadbald of Kent. Their daughter, Eanflaeda, had been born on Easter day (new calculation) and offered at once by her father for Christian baptism, since he had escaped a murder attempt that night. She thus became the first Christian in Northumbria; Edwin and the rest were baptised the next year in York Minster.[155] The baby Eanflaeda had been baptised by the Roman missionary Paulinus, a companion of Augustine. When Penda and Caedwalla ravaged Northumbria (633) and Edwin was killed, Aethelburgh and Paulinus took the family, including Eanflaeda and probably her cousin Hilda, and fled before the pagans to live in Kent and Gaul, where they continued to observe the new date for Easter.[156]

Some years later, Eanflaeda returned to Northumbria as the wife of Oswy. Their daughter was princess Alfleda, who as soon as she was weaned was given by her father to her kinswoman Hilda to be brought up at Whitby, as a thank-offering after his victory at the decisive battle of Winwead, 15 November 655.[157] While the whole experience of her mother had been rooted in the traditions of Gaul and Rome, by 664 Alfleda had lived for nine years in an Irish environment. There may have been no conflict about this, but when the question was raised, it is not at all likely that the queen would be content to continue to celebrate a different Easter from her daughter, especially since Easter, the day of her birth, was so significantly linked to the new Easter date. Later Eanflaeda joined Alfleda as a nun at Whitby, where her daughter

155 EH, Bk. 2: 14, p. 187.
156 EH, Bk. 2: 20, p. 205.
157 EH, Bk. 3: 24, p. 291.

succeeded Hilda as abbess. Quite apart from the domestic difficulties of two Easter days and two periods of Lent, there was not the slightest chance that the problem would be resolved by Eanflaeda changing her way of celebrating Easter.

The other family problem was posed by Alfleda's half-brother, Aldfrith. He had fought at his father's side at the Winwead as a good soldier, clever, able, and ambitious, but he was a man without secure prospects. He had been given some authority in Deira while Oswy was expanding the northern borders, but Aldfrith had his own way to make. It seems probable that he raised the question of the two dates of Easter in order to discredit his father in public and show him as provincial and wrong about Easter, therefore undermining his Christian alliances in Kent and Gaul. He brought in the young Wilfrid to propose the arguments for the new Easter dating, having him ordained priest by Agilbert just before the council. Disappointed in his schemes at Whitby, Aldfrith then married Cynburgh, sister of Peada of Mercia, and raised a rebellion in the same year; when that failed, he disappeared from history.[158]

It was not a matter of taking sides in a theological dispute which had caused the Northumbrian kings to follow the Irish dating of Easter. After the year of chaos following the death of Edwin, there was bitter warfare between the pagan invaders and the new Christian claimant to the throne, Oswald, who, like his brother and successor Oswy, had been in exile and received Christian baptism from Irish monks on Iona. Oswald became king in Northumbria, and naturally at once introduced missionaries from Iona, who followed the conservative Irish customs. In one year, and with disciples of Paulinus still alive and active, the new calculation for the date of Easter was surely still assumed to be correct

---

158 For another discussion of these issues, cf. Henry Mayr-Harting in *The Coming of Christianity to Anglo-Saxon England* (London, 1972), chap. 7, "The Synod of Whitby," pp. 103–13.

by many in Northumbria, but a difference came with the advent of the Irish-trained Oswald and Oswy and their new Irish missionaries, friends of the kings, who kept Easter as they had done on Iona, on a different day from the Roman missionaries, and indeed from the rest of the Church. The second stage in the conversion of Northumbria, therefore, accidentally differed from the first in this one matter. Paulinus, Edwin, Aethelburgh, and their daughter Eanflaed, later the wife of Oswy, naturally calculated according to the modern revised dating; Aidan and Oswald and Oswy equally naturally according to the unrevised dating, which had also originally come from Rome. It was an unconscious difference, but confusing for the Northumbrians.

The politics of Oswy are easy to understand. The problems with a divided Easter in his household were as nothing compared to the risk of losing the alliances which his marriage represented. That the decision reached at Whitby was fruitful was immediately shown when later in the same year Egbert of Kent, the queen's uncle, and Oswy jointly sent Wigheard to Rome to be ordained as the next archbishop of Canterbury. Pope Vitalian then wrote congratulating Oswy on his conformity about Easter, and mentioning warmly Eanfleda's part in the matter.[159] Oswy was well aware of latent problems concerning his wife and her relations in Kent and Gaul. He was no less alert to the possibility that his son could demonstrate through the debate that his father was concerned only with that area of Christianity in Northumbria dominated by Iona, while he himself would assert his wider alliances through Wilfrid. Well aware of issues quite other than the calculation of Easter Day, Oswy began the council with a reference to the need for unity throughout the whole Church. At the end, he turned the tables on his son by claiming the exact position Aldfrith had hoped to gain, speaking, as Eddius says, *subridens*, with a secret smile.

159 EH, Bk. 3: 29, pp. 319–23.

When Wilfrid had ended his speech, King Oswiu said, 'Is it true, Colman, that the Lord said these words to Peter?' Colman answered, 'It is true, O king. . . . Do you all agree, without any dispute, that these words were primarily addressed to Peter and that the Lord gave him the keys of the kingdom of heaven?' They both answered 'Yes'. Thereupon the king concluded, 'Then I tell you, that since he is the doorkeeper I will not contradict him . . . lest when I come to the gates of the kingdom of heaven there may be no-one to open them.'[160]

In matters of political alliance and credibility as high king on a large scale, Oswy was no one's fool. But with such undercurrents to manage, it was no wonder he had been rather thoughtful when the council opened.

The Synod of Whitby decided the actual issue of the date of Easter on spiritual authority rather than argument, but it was the details of the calendar, which was by no means foremost at the synod, which Bede drew out and explained. As he knew from Eusebius,[161] the date of Easter had occupied the mind of the early church. The council of Nicea had decreed that Easter should always be observed on a Sunday.[162] How to determine *which* Sunday had, however, remained a problem, to be solved by astronomers as much as by theologians and biblical scholars. In England there had been one initial clash between the Roman missionaries and the British—that is to say, the Welsh Christians. Augustine wrote to ask advice from Pope Gregory about his relationship with them and received the reply:

160 EH, Bk. 3: 25, p. 307.
161 Eusebius, *De Vita Constantini*, 3: 18 (85.26–37).
162 For the view of the Council of Nicea, cf. N. Tanner, *Decrees of the Ecumenical Councils*, vol. 1 (London: Sheed and Ward, 1990), p. 19.

We commit to you, my brother, all the bishops of Britain that the unlearned may be instructed, the weak strengthened by your counsel, and the perverse corrected by your authority.[163]

Augustine therefore invited the Welsh bishops to a conference and urged them: "that they should preserve catholic peace with him and undertake the joint labour of evangelizing the heathen for the Lord's sake."[164] After a long dispute, in which the calculation of the date of Easter was mentioned, "they were unwilling, in spite of the prayers, exhortations and rebukes of Augustine, and his companions, to give their assent, a stance which they maintained after a further long discussion, saying also that 'they would not preach the way of life to the English nation.'" The contacts between the Christians in Wales and the mission to the Anglo-Saxons seemed to have ceased thereafter. A demand for uniformity from a stance of power had resulted in deep and lasting division. At first the Welsh were simply old-fashioned in calculating Easter and therefore at variance with the more up-to-date tables from Rome, but as a result of the confrontation with Augustine, it became for them a sign of their individuality.

But with the Irish it was different, and any conflict over jurisdiction and the authority of Augustine did not flare up in his lifetime. In 664, over one hundred years after the coming of both Augustine and the Roman mission and Aidan and the Irish, a point of disagreement about the date at which Easter should be celebrated each year was seen to divide them; but it had in no way prevented joint evangelisation earlier. The golden age of Northumbria in the seventh and eighth centuries, one of the most amazing flowerings of Christian culture known, was based on an Anglo-Saxon Northumbria filled with Irish and with Roman missionaries, and in other kingdoms the contacts between them were also basic.

163 EH, Bk. 1: 27, pp. 87–89.
164 EH, Bk. 2: 2, p. 139.

It is a false dichotomy to see English and Irish in opposition in these early centuries. The true picture is of a pagan culture, that of the Anglo-Saxons, in touch with Christian culture in two ways, one from Rome through Gaul, one from Rome through Ireland. The southern Irish had already accepted the new calculations before Whitby. Why some of the Irish and also some of the English differed from the new missionaries about this crucial date was not a matter of alternative symbolism or theology or biblical study, but of the authority for the two calendric calculations. It was not, as Wilfrid suggested at Whitby, because the Irish were Quartodecimans—that is, those who kept the feast of Easter on any day of the week, provided it was the fourteenth of Nisan. The Irish calculated Easter in a perfectly orthodox manner; the problem was that they were using lunar tables which had reached them from Rome but had been replaced elsewhere. Other minor differences also caused the dates sometimes to coincide, sometimes to be a week apart, sometimes four weeks apart. To Anglo-Saxon Christians such differences had been by and large tolerable until the issue was raised, and after 664 they and most of the Irish agreed to observe together the new dating for Easter; by 731 even the conservative Iona had followed suit.

Why some of the Irish and also some of the English differed from the new Roman missionaries about this crucial date was a matter of their loyalty to the tradition of Columba, but behind it lay the more fundamental problem of calendric calculation. The question was about the date of the Paschal full moon after the Vernal Equinox, a combination of solar and lunar calendars which even electronic calculators cannot solve. This question was answered by the adoption of cycles of years. The first person to draw up such a cycle was Victorius of Aquitaine, whose work was adopted in Rome about 457. It comprised 532 years, starting with the supposed date of the crucifixion, and ran from AD 28 to AD 559. This cycle was improved upon by Dionysius Exiguus, who drew up a cycle which ran from 1 BC to AD 532 and from AD 532 to AD 1063. In 525 he had produced a table for calculating Easter based on the lunar cycle of 532 years—that is, twenty-eight periods of nineteen years each, reckoned from the year of the birth of Christ.[165] This was finally adopted by the Church, but it was not and still is not entirely satisfactory; Bede wrote extensively about the problems involved, but in his account of the debate at Whitby, calendric matters were not central, nor would they have been any more comprehensible to the court than they are to ourselves.

The results of the synod's decision were to determine the alliances and orientation of the Church in Britain, but there was no scapegoating of those who refused to change. Colman indeed resigned his bishopric and returned to his monastery, but in a sense he had no option; a monk and bishop holding his authority from Iona, he naturally returned there with some English and some Irish monks. He took with him some of the bones of Aidan, but also left some of them in Lindisfarne. Significantly, Oswy showed his respect for Colman by asking him to name his successor as bishop (Tuda) and as abbot (Eata). The chapter following Bede's account of Whitby was devoted to the highest praise of Colman as an apostolic servant of God.[166] Respect for Columba, Aidan, and Colman had surrounded the debate.

The community on Iona continued to keep the "true Easter of Columba."[167] Built as they were on the immense authority of the holiness of their saints, they were not moved by royal decrees from Whitby, nor changed by Ronan and Finan's debates; they were equally unmoved by Adamnan's arguments. But in 729 a very respected English Irish-trained monk, Egbert, voluntarily abandoned his way of life and

---

165 Admirably discussed by Faith Wallis, *Bede: The Reckoning of Time* (Liverpool: Liverpool University Press, 1999).

166 EH, Bk. 3: 26, pp. 309–11.

167 *Adamnan's Life of St Columba*, ed. and trans. A. O. Anderson and M. Anderson, (London: Nelson, 1962), Bk. 1: 3, p. 219.

went and lived humbly on Iona. Respect for him led to discussion, and he was able to show them why it was in line with their own traditions that they should change. He died on the first Easter day calculated in the new way to be celebrated on Iona—a change that had nothing to do with politics and everything to do with prayer, holiness, and humility.[168]

Issues are always more complex than doctrine only. There were domestic and political problems at the northern court. There were problems for mission in Northumbria, where the two dates for the Easter feast made differences about baptism. There were practical problems about the calendric calculations to be resolved. Bede, looking back at the debate, stressed what concerned him—that is, the unity of all round the Resurrection and the importance of astronomical calculations being correct. Time leading into eternity, non-time, nevertheless has its own dimensions, and these mattered. Numbers are as important as words.[169] But everyone involved, of different backgrounds and traditions, agreed in their devotion to Easter as the central feast of the Resurrection. With this basic unity in mind, they were able to discuss how they were to look towards Jesus as the risen Lord, and so they emerged from the debate without hating each other. Where those who differed from the majority of Christians did so in ignorance, while their conduct and prayer remained sound, Bede himself did not deal out condemnation. He wrote, for instance, of Aidan, his ideal among monks:

> All these things I greatly admire and love in this bishop. . . . I neither praise nor approve of him insofar as he did not observe Easter at the proper time. . . . I do approve of this, that in his celebration of Easter he had no other thought in his heart, he reverenced and preached no other doctrine than we do, namely the redemption of the human race by the passion, resurrection

168 EH, Bk. 5: 22, p. 555.
169 Cf. Alexander Murray in *Reason and Society in the Middle Ages* (Oxford, 1978), pp. 146–47.

and ascension into heaven of the one mediator between God and men even the man Jesus Christ.[170]

In conclusion, the meeting at Whitby shows that no divisive situation is ever resolved by discussion of divisive topics alone, but by the depth of love and prayer and respect for what already unites. It is perhaps not without interest to see how the outcome of this debate, with all its peculiarities, in fact imbued the Anglo-Saxons afterwards with a greater devotion than ever for the central and uniting fact of the Resurrection. As new converts, the Anglo-Saxons had not found the idea of a festival in spring entirely new, and they saw a connection between the date of the Pasch and their custom of celebrating a spring goddess; in his book on time, Bede refers to the Anglo-Saxon name for the feast of the Resurrection:

> Easter-month, which is now called the paschal month, was formerly so called from a goddess of theirs (the English) called Eostre and since her festival was celebrated then it had that name. By that name they now call the time of Pascha, customary observance giving its name to a new solemnity.[171]

The name has remained pagan, as indeed did the Anglo-Saxon word *Lent* (spring), which is still used rather than the Latin *jejunium* (the fast); the days of the week likewise did not become the series of ferias after the first day of Sunday, but remain obstinately dedicated to Woden, Thor, and Freya. The names remained, but in each case the content was radically different. Not the words but the content mattered; as Bede said, "I thank you, good Jesu, for turning us from such vanities, and allowing us to offer the sacrifice of praise." Not that the date of the death and resurrection of Jesus was a myth, or in any

170 EH, Bk. 3: 17, p. 267.
171 *Bede: The Reckoning of Time*, ed. and trans. Faith Wallis (Liverpool, 1999), cap. 15, pp. 53–54.

way arbitrary; it was an historical fact in time, and because of it, all time was changed into a new configuration. The date depended primarily on the Scriptures, but tradition had linked the date into the ebb and flow of the universe, of all creation, and it is not surprising to find that one of Bede's most intense passages on the calculation of Easter occurs in his commentary on the account of the creation of the world in Genesis. In his first book on the calculation of time, he linked the date of Easter with the created world in detail: the Pasch, he says, is central to creation as well as to redemption:

> When the equinox is passed, that the shadow of death may be vanquished by the true light, . . . in the first month of the year, which is called the month of New Fruits, so that the joy of a new life may be celebrated . . . at the turn of the moon, to show how the glory of the mind is turned from earthly things to heavenly ones . . . on the Lord's Day, when the light shows the triumph of Christ and our own resurrection.[172]

To secure unity which flowered into uniformity was not the same as imposing uniformity; and whatever the superficial motives and schemes of those present may have been, the true unity forged at Whitby was a turning point indeed for Anglo-Saxon Christianity. An incipient difference, which could have been used by secular ambitions, was resolved by patience and respect all round, so that unity about what mattered most could eventually produce a true uniformity. The proof of this is to be found in the continued English love of Easter, which produced a flowing of energy from the Resurrection into art, drama, and poetry:

---

172 Bede, *De Temporibus* cap. xv, "On the Sacrament of the Paschal Season," BOD, 123a., p. 599.

For at the dawning there came a throng of angels,

the rapture of those hosts surrounded the Saviour's tomb,

The earthly vault was opened,

the Prince's corpse received the breath of life;

the ground shook and hell's inhabitants rejoiced.

The young man awoke dauntless from the earth;

the mighty Majesty arose, victorious and wise.[173]

II
The Problems of the Easter Controversy in the Writings of the Venerable Bede
A SIMPLIFIED GUIDE

A. Bede's Discussion of the Date of Easter

Ecclesiastical History of the English People, Book 3, cap. xxv: Arguments used at the Council of Whitby. Book 5, cap. xxi: Letter of Ceolfrith to Nechtan, king of the Picts.

Commentary on Genesis, 17–18: commenting on the creation of the sun and moon, pp. 15–20.

Commentary on Luke, VI, xxii, 7–8 (p. 375).

Commentary on Mark, IV, xiv, 12 (p. 609).

De Temporum Ratione, caps. v, viii, xix, lxiv.

De Temporibus: full discussion of Paschal calculation.

De Natura Rerum, ix–xiv (pp. 206–99).

Letter to Wicthed, xi (p. 324).

---

173 *Anglo-Saxon Poetry,* "The Descent into Hell," trans. S. A. J. Bradley, Everymans Library (London: Dent, 1982), p. 392.

B. Methods of Calculating Easter in Eighth-Century Northumbria

Points of Agreement

1. Easter must be celebrated on a Sunday.
2. It must fall in the first lunar month of the year.
3. It must be after the Vernal Equinox, i.e., the day in the solar year when the number of hours of daylight equal the hours of darkness after which the hours of daylight increase.
4. It must be after the first full moon after the Vernal Equinox.

Points of Difference

1. XIV Nisan

Romans: This was the day the Jews celebrated Passover, whatever the day of the week. It was not permissible to celebrate a Sunday as Easter if the Passover also occurred on that day; it was deferred to the next Sunday.

Celts: It was permissible to celebrate Easter on a Sunday on which Passover was also celebrated. Every seventh year this could result in the difference of a week between the two Easter celebrations.

2. The Vernal Equinox

Romans kept it on March 21st.

Celts kept it on March 25th.

3. The first full moon after the Vernal Equinox

FIRST DIFFERENCE:

Romans: The Paschal moon was that which became full after March 21st; if the moon was full before March 21st, that was not deemed to be the Paschal moon and the next lunar month was then regarded as the first month of the year and that moon as the Paschal moon.

Celts: The Paschal moon was the one full after March 25th.

SECOND DIFFERENCE:

Romans: They began the liturgical day on the evening before, so the Sunday after the full moon after the Vernal Equinox (March 21st) was not regarded as Easter Day if the full moon occurred after midnight; in this case Easter would be celebrated on the next Sunday, a week later.

Celts: They began each day in the morning, so if the full moon after the Vernal Equinox rose at any time on the night of Saturday to Sunday, the Celts would keep that Sunday as Easter.

THEREFORE:

Romans: Possible days in the lunar month for Easter were xv–xxi Nisan. Possible days in the year for Easter Day were March 22–April 25.

Celts: Possible days of the lunar month for Easter were xiv–xx Nisan. Possible days of the year for Easter Day were March 24–April 22.

C. Examples

1. Romans and Celts might celebrate Easter **on the same day** when, for example, the new moon was March 12th (Thursday) and the full moon March 26th (Wednesday). The Vernal Equinox was either March 21st or March 25th. Therefore, Easter Day would be the first Sunday after the full moon after the Equinox, which for both would be March 30th.

2. They might celebrate Easter **a week apart** when, for example, the new moon was March 19th (Saturday) and the full moon April 2nd, which fell on Sunday after midnight. The Vernal Equinox was either March 21st or March 25th. Celtic Easter would be April 2nd, the same night; Roman Easter would be April 9th, a week later.

3. They might celebrate Easter **four weeks apart** when, for example, the new moon was March 8th (Sunday), and the full moon March 22nd (Friday). Vernal Equinox was either March 21st or March 25th. As the full moon came *after* the Roman Vernal Equinox of March 21st, the Roman Easter would be the following Sunday, March 24th. But the full moon would be *before* the Celtic Vernal Equinox of March 25th, so this would not be for them the first full moon after the Vernal Equinox. They would, therefore, not count that as the month Nisan but wait for the next new moon to be full and would celebrate four weeks later. Celtic Easter would be April 21st.

Note: If Passover was celebrated on a Sunday of the first full moon after March 25th, the Celts would postpone Easter for a week.

(The present differences between Orthodox Easter and Western Easter depend upon the choice of the Julian Calendar or the Gregorian Calendar, where there is a fourteen-day difference in calculating the Vernal Equinox.)

5
ANSELM *of* CANTERBURY
A MONASTIC SCHOLAR

◆ ■ ◆ ■ ◆ ■ ◆ ■ ◆ ■ ◆ ■ ◆ ■ ◆

I

In the year 1109, on the Wednesday in Holy Week, the archbishop of Canterbury lay dying. His friends, knowing that they were at the death-bed of a saint, were ready to improve the occasion: "My lord and father," they said, "we cannot help knowing that you are going to leave the world to be at the Easter court of your king."[174] But Anselm was not to be caught by pieties and sentimentalities. His reply is the key to his life and a way to begin to understand him: "And indeed," he replied, "if His will is set upon this I will gladly obey His will. However, if He would prefer me to stay among you, at least until I can settle a question about the origin of the soul which I am turning over in my mind, I should welcome this with gratitude, for I do not know whether anyone will solve it when I am dead."

There is in this reply first the obedience of the monk—a joyful love of whatever might be God's will for him; and secondly, a true estimate of his own intellectual powers as a scholar, without false humility—a mind still employed to its utmost in understanding the things of God for the sake of the people of God. From that starting point I would like to make some comments on Anselm as a monastic scholar and man of prayer in the belief that his way of doing theology is relevant to our own situation. But before proceeding to his ideas, perhaps I should fill

---

174 *Vita Anselmi* by Eadmer, II, lxvii. The references to this source, abbreviated as *VA*, are to book and chapter and may be found in R.W. Southern's edition, reprinted in Oxford Medieval Texts, 1972.

in the background of his life, since it is essential to my argument that his monastic life cannot be separated from his ideas and theology.

Seventy-six years earlier Anselm had been born in Aosta in northern Italy. As a young man he left home and came north into the turbulent, changing society of eleventh-century Europe, eager to learn and equipped with one of the most powerful and original minds of the age—or of any age. For three years he seems to have wandered about northern Europe, presumably visiting the great centres of monastic and liturgical life, at Cluny and Fleury, as well as the monastic schools which were still centres of intellectual experiment before the rise of the secular schools and universities.

Eventually, says his biographer and disciple, Eadmer, "he went to Normandy, to see, to talk to, and to stay with a certain master by the name of Lanfranc."[175] This was the beginning of Anselm's association with the monastery of Bec, where Lanfranc was prior. He left it thirty-four years later to become archbishop of Canterbury. It was during these years as monk, prior, and abbot of Bec that Anselm began to write, and his first works were by no means immature or experimental. It was then that he wrote the *Prayers and Meditations*, the *Monologion*, and, above all, the *Proslogion*. Later, as archbishop of Canterbury, Anselm wrote only "in great tribulation of heart." The greatest of his theological works does indeed belong to that period, the *Cur Deus Homo?*, but it was completed only in the peace of exile, not in the constant pressures of controversy and bickerings at home.

As archbishop he was an administrator first, a scholar perforce second, and he was regretfully aware of this. To his monks at Canterbury he said: "Just as an owl is glad when she is in her nest with her chicks and . . . all is well with her . . . so it is with me. For when I am with you, all is well with me, and this is the joy and consolation of my

175 *VA*, I, v.

life. But when I am separated from you, and my ways lie among men who are in the world, then I am torn this way and that by the onrush of disputes of many kinds and I am harassed by secular disputes of many kinds which I hate."[176] His words leave no room for doubt about where his preference lay, but that does not mean that he did his work as archbishop grudgingly. As far as the "secular disputes" were concerned, he had one very simple expedient for dealing with them, "for," says his biographer, "when he was in a crowd of litigants, while his opponents were laying their heads together . . . he would compose himself, in the sweet quietness of a pure heart, to sleep."[177] As archbishop, however, he was alert and discerning in all that pertained to Church affairs.

Anselm was to occupy a central place in public affairs in England in the second half of his life, but it was the cloister that had really set free his most creative abilities. At Bec he was the spiritual master, the monastic scholar *par excellence*, and it is in the writings of that period that it is easiest to see what it meant for Anselm to be a monk and a scholar, with the entire commitment of the monastic life combined with the integrity of scholarship of the highest kind.

II

Eadmer tells us that Anselm noticed the similarity of the disciplines of study and monasticism. As a pupil of Lanfranc, Anselm "wearied his body with late nights, with cold and with hunger because of his studies, and so he began to think that if he became a monk he would not have to put up with anything more severe than he was now suffering, nor would he lose the reward of his labour."[178] This is not, of course, the highest possible motive for religious vocation, and the fact that Eadmer records it points to his having heard of it from Anselm, who

176 *VA*, II, viii.
177 *VA*, I, xxvii.
178 *VA*, I, v.

was never one for illusions about himself. The account of his choice of Bec must similarly have come from the saint himself: not, he decided, Cluny, where liturgy would prevent him from studying; and he was dubious about Bec, "because there the outstanding ability of Lanfranc will condemn me to insignificance."[179] Again, not a pious outlook, but with all its imperfections one which showed his basic honesty; he knew he could never play second fiddle in intellectual matters, and he could admit it plainly.

It is interesting to note in passing that Anselm did not immediately choose the monastic way of life of the great Benedictine house. He hesitated, and the alternatives he considered are symptomatic of that age. He thought first of becoming a hermit, one of the major attractions in the next hundred years; and then of becoming a secular land-holder on his estates, serving the poor—a remarkable anticipation of later forms of Christian life and devotion.

In the end he settled the matter in a way which was typical of him: he acted under obedience to another, and obeyed implicitly what his advisor (Lanfranc) told him to do: he became a monk at Bec. Within three years Lanfranc had gone to Caen, and Anselm was appointed prior; and at the death of the abbot and founder, Herluin, Anselm became abbot. Thus for thirty-three years he lived at Bec under the Rule of St. Benedict as interpreted in a Norman monastery of the eleventh century with the full weight of liturgical observance. During that time he wrote the *Prayers and Meditations*, his most directly spiritual work; the *Monologion*; the *Proslogion*, one of the greatest of all philosophical works; *De Grammatico; De Veritate; De Libertate Arbitrii; De Casu Diaboli*; and the *Epistola de Incarnatione Verbi*—about half of all his works. And he wrote them not in spite of but because of his monastic commitment.

179 *VA*, I, v.

How did all these writings form part of his monastic life? The clue I think is in the *Vita Anselmi* in which Eadmer says: "From that time on he gave himself up entirely to being a true monk, and to understanding the rational basis of the monastic life and expounding it to others."[180] These three points seem to form the ground of Anselm's understanding of his vocation as a monk and scholar, and I would like to take them in turn.

First: "he gave himself up entirely to being a true monk." Anselm's concept of monastic life has to be gleaned from his statements in his letters, in records of private conversations, and from some of the *Prayers*. The most important of the letters in which Anselm discusses the monastic life is the one he sent to the monk Lanzo at Cluny in 1072. He himself considered this letter to contain his true opinion of monastic life, later recommending a monk of Canterbury to read it, while Eadmer quoted it in the *Vita* as typical of Anselm's position on monasticism. It is the letter of a monastic conservative *par excellence*; there is no trace of discontent with the intellectual and spiritual atmosphere of monasticism as he experienced it. "Let him rejoice at finding himself where he can at last remain for the whole of his life, not unwillingly but voluntarily, driving away all thought of removal so that he may quietly give himself up to the exercises of a pious life . . . let him refuse to pass judgement on the customs of the place even if they seem useless."[181] And more directly to Lanzo: "Devote your whole strength to attaining peace of mind . . . which is not attained by any monk without constancy and forbearance . . . or without a studious and devout observance of all the customs of the monastery, even if their purpose is not clear."

This is the framework out of which came ways of thought and of prayer which revolutionised medieval theology and devotion. And they

180   *VA*, I, xxi.
181   *VA*, I, xx.

did not come out of it as a protest but as a natural and right growth. Anselm loved being a monk; accepting and being formed by monastic ways was to him a matter not only of duty but of joy. To Helinandus he wrote of monastic life as *pondus cantabile*—a weight that is borne singing. The monk, he insisted elsewhere, is the man who instead of being able to give God merely the fruits of the tree, has given him the tree itself.

Anselm's concept of the monastic life was a part of his general way of thinking, not an exception to it as though he had never tried to apply his mind to it. It is in line with his other ideas—for instance, his idea of truth as that which corresponds to what really and objectively is, rather than to the thought in the mind of the speaker. His concept of freedom is similar: freedom does not lie in the ability to choose between good and evil, but in the ability to choose always what is right. "The ability to keep uprightness of will (*rectitudo*) for its own sake is the complete definition of freedom of choice." Likewise, for Anselm, sin is not to be assessed by a psychological standard but by a theological one: "How can any sin be called small," he asks, "when it is an offence against God?" His definitions are always vertical, not horizontal. They define man in relation to God, and they have as much to do with theories of similitude and likeness, image and symbol, as with theories of cause and effect. So, in relation to monastic life, authenticity was not to be judged by personal approval or disapproval of monastic customs; "even if their purpose is not clear" the customs were to be followed. They were seen, in fact, as converting ordinances by which a man could be changed and shaped. It is, as we shall see later, the same encounter that Anselm suggests in the *Proslogion*.

Like the Greek Fathers, Anselm believed that man is created in the image of God, and his whole purpose is to have this image restored so that he can again perfectly reflect this truth that is in God. But the image is not reflected truly in man; it has been distorted by sin. And for Anselm the monastic life is the way of restoring that image defaced by the disobedience of sin. In the "Prayer to St. John the Baptist" Anselm says:

> You fashioned your gracious image in me, and I superimposed upon it the image that is hateful . . . refashion the face I have spoiled, restore the innocence I have violated.

This is the key to Anselm's approach to monasticism, which seems at first sight far from our way of thinking. He would not have said, for instance, that the monastic way of life is the expression of an individual's understanding of God's call to him, or that its authenticity depends upon the external actions being the direct fruit of that understanding. For Anselm, monastic life, like other things, existed in its highest degree in the mind of God, and was reflected in man, who is God's image. But the image was marred by sin, and so there is a gap, a discrepancy between the ideal and the actual which can be remedied only by a continuing experience of the detailed reality of monastic life which can remove and remedy the deformed image. The monastic life is an ideal to which the monk is to be conformed. This leads Anselm to lay great stress on the externals of religious life, especially upon the habit. To his mind no one who had worn the habit, even if they had never intended to take vows, could leave the monastic life without apostasy. This was clearly his opinion in his letters to the Princess Gunhilda and her cousin Mathilda, neither of whom had made religious vows, though they had worn the habit. He refers to them both as "lost daughters," and sees every step away from the cloister as taking them along the road to damnation. The habit was to him sacramental: "The black and heavy clothes remind the monk that he is a sinner; they cover him from head to feet to turn him to this thought from the beginning to the end of life; they present also the form of the cross and re-establish in him the passion of the Lord; the crown of hair left by the tonsure tells that the monk is both priest and king."[182]

The monastic life was a practical affair for Anselm, a matter of actually doing certain things, not just thinking various thoughts. It was, as it were, an icon through which a man came to the reality it represented. An icon and not an idol, for he was equally aware that monastic customs were not an end in themselves. "To wear the religious habit serves no purpose unless at the same time an effort is made to be interiorly what one appears to be."[183] It is the way through, not the end. In his "Prayer to St. Benedict," this is also the theme:

> I profess to lead a life of continual turning to God, as I promised by taking the name and habit of a monk, but my long life cries out against me, and my conscience convicts me as a liar to God and angels and men. . . . I profess myself a soldier, a scholar, a monk, but my life cries out that I am a liar.

Again, in the "Prayer for Any Abbot," he says: "They behold me preceded like an abbot but I do not behold that I live like an abbot." The monk for Anselm was *peccator monachus*—a sinner in need of the mercy of God. This sense of shortcoming, of sin, of alienation, is present in all the prayers, and the solution in each is to turn towards the mercy of God. By one's coming gradually into relation with God the image is restored, and then the truth perceived by the heart and expressed by the lips will fully correspond to the truth as it really is in God.

---

182 *Liber Anselmi Archiepiscopi de Humanis Moribus per Similitudines,* chaps. 92 and 93. In *Memorials of St Anselm,* ed. R. W. Southern and F. S. Schmitt (London, 1969), p. 78.
183 Ibid., chap. 96, p. 79.

III

For Anselm, an essential part of this process of conversion was an intellectual one. The intellect is an integral part of man's created being and needs, as much as the rest of him, to be brought into contact with God for restoration and cleansing. "To discover the rational basis of the monastic life" is the second part of Eadmer's statement about Anselm's concerns. "The rational basis"—what did Anselm mean by "*ratio*"? To find out one looks rather at the *Monologion* and the *Proslogion* than at the *Prayers*. The first title Anselm gave to the *Monologion* was *De ratione fidei*, an ambiguous title which he soon dropped. More appropriate for what he was trying to do was his sub-title, *Fides quaerens intellectum*, for the *Proslogion*—that treatise in which prayer and intellectual thought are most wonderfully combined. It is here that we can see what Anselm meant by "*ratio*," and how it formed part of his prayer.

The *Proslogion* begins as a meditation:

> Come now, little man,
> > turn aside for a while from your daily employment,
> > escape for a moment from the tumult of your thoughts.
> > > Put aside your weighty cares,
> > > let your burdensome distractions wait,
> > > free yourself awhile for God
> > > and rest awhile in him.
> Enter the inner chamber of your soul,
> > shut everything out except God
> > and that which can help you in seeking him,
> > and when you have shut the door, seek him.
> Now, my whole heart, say to God,
> > 'I seek your face,
> > Lord, it is your face I seek'.[184]

---

184 *Proslogion*, chap. 1, ll. 1–14. In *The Prayers and Meditations of St Anselm*, trans. into modern English by Benedicta Ward, SLG, and published by Penguin Classics, 1973. This quotation is from p. 239.

It is clear that the major part of the *Proslogion*—twenty-one chapters out of twenty-five—is a meditation, a prayer reflecting upon the nature of belief in God. But to look only at those is to side-step the issue, for the early chapters contain a philosophic statement about the existence and nature of God more exciting than any produced in a monastery before or since and which has, more than anything else, given to Anselm—mistakenly—the title "Father of Scholasticism." It is a demonstration which has aroused, and continues to arouse, lively interest among philosophers and theologians, including Descartes, Kant, Hegel, Leibnitz, and Barth. Indeed, one might almost say it takes giants to misunderstand a giant, and it is interesting to note in this connection that R. W. Southern in his book *Saint Anselm and His Biographer* says: "It may be claimed that a share of philosophical naïveté is an aid to understanding his [Anselm's] thought."

"God is that than which nothing greater can be thought." It is important to see this in context and not in isolation, and especially in the context of its first expression. At Bec Anselm was exercising all the abilities of his mind to discover "the rationale of the nature of God as the true faith holds it to be," when suddenly "one night during mattins the grace of God shone in his heart, the whole matter became clear to his mind, and a great joy and jubilation filled his whole being."[185] It was a matter of illumination about what was already believed, and it is this that provided the starting point for his arguments, not the reverse. It happened in the middle of a monastic service, and the whole setting of it is a prayer of longing and desire for God which is entirely monastic in tone. There is a joy and excitement which is far removed from the logical demonstrations of scholasticism and closer to the mystical experience of prayer. Anselm was not constructing a logical structure and imposing it upon God; nor was he proposing to discover

185 *VA*, I, xix.

by logical argument the existence of God as the end term of his own propositions. His fundamental way of doing theology was to bring all the powers of his mind to bear upon what he already believed, and this experience at Bec produced the gift of understanding more.

It has often been said that the "proofs" of the *Proslogion* would never convince an unbeliever. For Anselm, theology is only true insofar as it corresponds to the being of God, and *"ratio"* for him is *"ratio Dei,"* the living Word of God which is beyond all systems of human thought. Applying to the utmost all the powers of intellect and reason to "seeking God," the basis is nonetheless a confrontation with God himself and his saving purposes, which will in itself clear the mind of its darkness and restore it to that contact with God in himself which can be described either as true theology or as prayer. To do this Anselm uses every kind of concept: the Scriptures, dogma, and credal statements on the one hand, the secular concepts of philosophy on the other. "God is that than which nothing greater can be thought" affirms the impossibility of proving the unknowable essence of God by human reasoning. It is a way of knowledge that is apophatic; it is a demonstration rather than a proof. And from it Anselm explores whatever can be said or thought about God, using this first insight as the basis of his prayer and thought. "Thank you, good Lord," he exclaims, "for by your gift I first believed and now by your illumination I understand."

This encounter with God, which he calls "illumination," is the attitude of a monk who, having dedicated his entire being to God, offers the whole of his mind, as well as his body, to knowing that truth which is beyond concepts, and to receiving it as a transfiguring experience. This is how Anselm understood the "rational basis" of the monastic life—not by looking for reasons to justify it, but by seeing the truth in God.

IV

The mystics tell us that no experience of God remains static or unused; it must communicate itself. This leads to the third of Eadmer's points about Anselm: "He expounded it to others."

Anselm was not primarily a teacher, a school-man, a pedagogue, although some of his advice—on education for example—was not bettered until the late nineteenth century. He was concerned with his personal search for God, and it is significant that he used the dynamic word *seek*. For Anselm prayer was not a static reception of something that could be passed on to others, but an ardent and vigorous quest in which others might join him if they wished. The end of the *Proslogion* is his fullest expression of this attitude:

> God of truth,
>
> I ask that I may receive,
>
> so that my joy may be full.
>
> Meanwhile, let my mind meditate on it,
>
> let my tongue speak of it,
>
> let my heart love it,
>
> let my mouth preach it,
>
> let my soul hunger for it,
>
> my flesh thirst for it,
>
> and my whole being desire it,
>
> until I enter into the joy of my Lord,
>
> who is God, one and triune, blessed forever. Amen.[186]

Looking back on his long life, Anselm placed his first understanding of prayer very early indeed. Born in 1033 near Mount St. Bernard,

---

186 *Proslogion,* chap. 26, ll. 786–97, pp. 266–67. (See n. 11.)

Anselm was a child of the mountains, and it was here that he first learned to be articulate about what was to be his way of prayer throughout his life. When he was archbishop in Canterbury, he used to talk about himself with his friends, such as the monks Eadmer, Alexander, and Baldwin, and on one occasion he told them how as a little boy he had believed that God lived on the snow-topped mountains above his home, and how in a dream he had set out to climb, passing on the way some lazy servants of the Lord whom the child blamed for their idle work; going upward, he met the Lord, who was attended by one of his servants and was able to sit and talk with him, beginning with dialogue about his own identity ("who he was, where he came from, what he wanted"), until he was ready to receive the "whitest of bread" in peace and communion.[187]

This story contained the whole of the Anselmian method. The sense of something amiss, incomplete, which as a child he saw in the idleness of servants, later became not blame of others but self-accusation and repentance; self-examination continued to be the basis of his prayers. The presence of other servants with him before God was always vital to his understanding of prayer with the saints as his friends; and that early longing for something beyond himself became a lifetime of striving for a dynamic ascent to God. His prayers followed this pattern of desire, self-knowledge, and repentance, leading into the joy of entering into the presence of God and conversing with him as a friend. When, in 1061, he became a Benedictine monk in the abbey of Bec and wrote his first brilliant works (including the immensely influential treatise called the *Proslogion,* and also most of his *Prayers and Meditations*), this pattern shaped them all.

He shared his way of prayer by sending copies of his own prayers to certain people and by giving some guidance about how to use them.

187 Eadmer, *Vita S. Anselmi,* ed. and trans. R. W. Southern, Nelson's Medieval Texts (Oxford, 1962), Bk. 1, cap. 111, pp. 5–6.

It was a personal and individual matter, not the setting up of a "school of spirituality." But from this intimate communication between the few came a whole new concept of meditative, solitary prayer in the inner chamber. Some of Anselm's ideas about praying are found in the preface he wrote to the collection of *Prayers and Meditations*:

> The purpose of the prayers and meditations that follow is to stir up the mind of the reader to the love or fear of God, or to self-examination. They are not to be read in a turmoil, but quietly, not skimmed or hurried through, but taken a little at a time with deep and thoughtful meditation.
>
> The reader should not trouble about reading the whole of any of them, but only as much as, by God's help, he finds useful in stirring up his spirit to pray, or as much as he likes. Nor is it necessary for him always to begin at the beginning, but wherever he pleases.
>
> With this in mind the sections are divided into paragraphs so that the reader can begin and leave off wherever he chooses; in this way he will not get bored with too much material but will be able to ponder more deeply those things that make him want to pray.[188]

He wrote in a similar way to the Princess Adelaide and the Countess Mathilda, perhaps an indication of the important part played by great and noble ladies in the development of devotion. They had the time and the leisure, as well as the inclination and ability, for spiritual adventure and were in a position to put the ideas of their spiritual masters into practice.

The *Proslogion* was also a prayer, an "*exemplum meditandi*," and it was written, Anselm says, to share with others the joy he had felt in his experience of God. His concern was that everyone, even the "fool,"

188 *Prayers and Meditations*, p. 89, n. 11.

should be brought to some experience of God whose nature it is to desire to bring sinners to repentance. Anselm's teaching always had this connotation of enabling others to experience God for themselves. He was not, like Lanfranc, a master of the schools, attracting pupils from outside the monastery and teaching them according to a system. Anselm preferred to talk with his friends, with a few intelligent monks, with whom he could discuss ideas and communicate by talking rather than by teaching.

This small group of lively and intelligent minds recurred throughout Anselm's life, whether in the monastic group of Lanfranc and Gundulf at Bec; or in the international circle of eminent men such as Hugh of Cluny, Peter Damian, Hugh of Grenoble, Pope Calixtus II, Anselm of Laon; or in that other group of more personal friends in England, Gilbert Crispin, Eadmer, Ralph of Battle, and the monks Baldwin and Alexander. It was in the small group exchanging ideas that Anselm was most at home, not in the debating hall. He was a great friend, as his letters also show, and it was as one sharing experience rather than as a master teaching disciples that Anselm communicated his knowledge. He talked with men "so that they may form themselves in the image of the spiritual man," and as a spiritual father Anselm was pre-eminent.

This is a side of him which has left, of its nature, little record, but Eadmer assures us it was for his spiritual wisdom and insight that Anselm was most valued both at Bec and Canterbury. In the monastery "all loved him as a very dear father"; "any with a private trouble hastened to unburden themselves to him as if to the gentlest of mothers." Like Aelred of Rievaulx, Anselm could be called a mother as well as a father in his care of his community, and this mothering side of his nature reflected the contemplative, receptive, caring aspect, just as the brilliant intellect and clear thought belonged to his fatherhood—a parallel which he himself draws in detail in his "Prayer to St. Paul":

Therefore you are fathers by your effect

and mothers by your affection.

Fathers by your authority, mothers by your kindness.

Fathers by your teaching, mothers by your mercy.[189]

Outside the monastery "he received all who came to him
with a gracious readiness and replied helpfully to them all . . . his
conversation drew all men to him in friendship and affection . . .
everyone who could enjoy his conversation was ready to do so, for on
any subject they wished he had heavenly counsel ready for them."[190]
This is surely the true monastic scholar who shares his insight with
others as the fruit of his contemplation of God; he is one through
whom a knowledge of God can be reached rather than someone wise
in his own right.

V

The picture I have tried to present of Anselm as a monastic scholar
is one which could only have emerged in the last century—perhaps
only in the last decades of the century. Within a few years of his death
Anselm's work suffered in various ways. He left no school of disciples,
only a few friends who had been influenced by him but who then went
their own way. His greatest work, the *Proslogion*, seems to have been
virtually unknown in the twelfth century, and Thomas Aquinas knew it
only at second hand and in a distorted form in the thirteenth. Fashions
of thought changed rapidly, and the formation of scholasticism soon
held the ground in Europe. It was only by careful selection, much later,
that scholars could begin to look back and call Anselm the Father of
Scholasticism, and by then his theology was seen through ways of
thought alien to his own.

189 *Prayers and Meditations*, Prayer to St. Paul, ll. 421–24, p. 154.
190 *VA*, II, ix.

In the realm of devotion, the genuine prayers of Anselm were at once lost to sight among a vast amount of similar material, most of it inferior. The prayers generated a school of spirituality and so found countless imitators. The corpus grew, all of it going under the name of Anselm, until the vast collection was published by Migne in the nineteenth century. At the beginning of the last century the work of Dom André Wilmart, in testing the authenticity of the Anselmian writings, prepared the way for Dom Schmitt's definitive edition in the 1960s. The prayers which are now regarded as genuinely by Anselm number nineteen, the meditations only three, which enables a much clearer picture to emerge of Anselm as a spiritual writer and guide. It is possible now to ask certain questions about Anselm as a spiritual writer and to discover in what way the impact of his teaching can be described as "the Anselmian revolution." Now that we have discussed the approach of Anselm to monastic life and learning, the remainder of this chapter will concern Anselm's contribution to Christian spirituality, first in his own day and then among the masters of the spiritual life.

The ethos of prayer in which Anselm was formed had changed little in the previous two centuries. It was basically a monastic devotion, for people outside the monasteries as well as for the monks. The central part that monasticism played in Anselm's life has already been noticed, and it only remains to emphasise the way in which the details of monastic life under the Rule of St. Benedict permeated Anselm's prayers. Take for instance, the Prologue to the Rule itself:

> Hearken, my son, to the precepts of the master and incline the ear of thine heart . . . by the labour of obedience return to him from whom thou hast strayed by the sloth of disobedience . . . and first of all whatever good work thou dost undertake, ask him with most instant prayer to perfect it . . . as we progress in

the monastic life and in faith, our hearts shall be enlarged and
we shall run with the unspeakable sweetness of love in the way
of God's commandments . . . we shall share by patience in the
sufferings of Christ, that we may deserve to be partakers also of
his kingdom.[191]

The life of the monk is seen here as a perpetual conversion, a
turning from the kingdom of sin and alienation towards the kingdom
of God and union with him; the way is that behind all the devotions
of Anselm, and, as we shall see, the movement from sin and fear
to love and desire through the sufferings of Christ is central to his
thought. In the "Prayer to St. Benedict" and the "Prayer for Any
Abbot," there are also clear echoes of the Rule. There are the same
images, the shepherd and sheep, the master and disciples, the father
and sons. There is also the figure of Christ behind the figure of the
abbot; the weight of solemn duty carried out in the shadow of the
judgement seat of Christ is exactly the picture St. Benedict draws of
the work of an abbot or monk. What Anselm adds is the personal
note of awareness of insufficiency for the human being within the
role, the feeling of being a hypocrite, of claiming things far above one's
ability. This is a part of a self-awareness new in the twelfth century.

As for St. Benedict, so for Anselm, prayer was based on the Bible and
the liturgy, and in each case it was expected that individuals would extend
this for themselves. For both, "mind and voice" were to be "in accord";[192]
prayer should be made "with tears and fervour of heart";[193] "in purity of
heart and tears of compunction."[194] But where St. Benedict sees private
prayer as being "brief and in the oratory,"[195] Anselm insists that one should
withdraw to a solitary place and pray there as long as one desires.

---

191 *Rule of St Benedict*, ed. and trans. Justin McCann (London, 1952), Prologue, pp. 7–13.
192 Ibid., chap. 19, p. 69.
193 Ibid., chap. 20, p. 69.
194 Ibid.
195 Ibid., chap. 52, p. 119.

Within the Benedictine life at Bec there was the Divine Office, the Mass, and the para-liturgical ceremonies of the Customary. The Office according to St. Benedict offered a framework of prayer based on the corporate recitation of the psalter, interspersed with readings from the rest of the Bible at various intervals during the day and night. During the tenth century, extra prayers had been added to this framework. The accretions with which centuries had surrounded the Office were still mainly in the nature of extra psalms.

The psalter was the prayer book *par excellence* of the monk; its familiar recurring phrases shaped the subconscious as well as the conscious mind, creating in the monk the attitudes of repentance and need, rejoicing and praise. It was also the prayer book of those of the laity who could read; the psalms could equally be learnt by heart by the devout among the non-literate. Any great lord or lady would want extracts from the psalter if they were at all inclined to piety. The earliest of Anselm's prayers were written as an appendix to just such a selection from the psalms made at the request of a great lady of pious habits.

Other prayers were made at the request of monks as well as for secular friends. It seems, therefore, that the austerity of the psalter was already wearing thin for monks as well as for laymen; a movement towards the personal, the interior, the subjective, was taking place in the eleventh and twelfth centuries, and its effect was felt on the use of the psalms.

The psalter is a difficult prayer book for Christians to use; Augustine had popularised a Christological interpretation of the psalms, and the influence of his great sermons on the psalms made them acceptable. The use of the Gloria Patri at the end of each also reminded the worshipper of the Christian setting of the Jewish prayers. The psalms are most easily used in an objective, corporate way—in fact, in recitation in choir. But already in the eleventh century the need was felt to draw out and make explicit their Christian application. This was often done by attaching brief, collect-type prayers to the end of each psalm, which would take up one or more themes from the psalm and give it both a Christian interpretation and a personal application to those using it.

Anselm's prayers are naturally full of the phrases of the psalms since he was formed by them, but the pattern of his prayers is along the lines of the psalter-collects, only drawn to great length. It seems to me that one might look for the source of this tendency in the hermit movement of the eleventh and twelfth centuries. Increasing numbers of men and women were praying alone; and using the psalms alone in a cell is completely different from their corporate recitation in choir. The stirrings towards this more personal prayer with the psalms came from the hermit orders in Italy—from Peter Damian, John Gualbert, and, in a rather different sense, John of Fécamp.

Thirdly, for the monk of Bec, there was the veneration of the saints. The Kalendar provided a liturgy for the saints throughout the year. Here again, Anselm received a tradition and expanded it. The devotion of the Carolingians was to God through Christ in the Spirit; it was permissible to invoke the prayers of those saints known from the Gospel, above all St. Mary. The austere phrases of the litany of the saints was the basis for this: "Holy Mary, pray for us." But already by the time of Anselm a warmer devotion was being felt towards the saints, in particular towards Mary as the one closest to the Lord. The grave, restrained prayers to her, basically the *Ave Maria*, were expanded into something more personal and expressive. The *O singularis merita* by Maurillus of Rouen is one instance of this.

Anselm took up this approach to the saints and expanded it into a kind of devotional psychology of holy persons, entering into dialogue with them, displaying an interest in their history, eager for their understanding—in particular St. Mary, to whom he addressed three long prayers, and the biblical saints, Peter, Paul, John, Stephen, and John Baptist. Also Nicolas, a saint of special interest in Normandy and St. Benedict, patron of monks.

Thus the idea of prayers said aloud and in conjunction with others was already shaping itself towards the idea of prayers said alone and in the heart. Here the tradition was met by the ancient tradition of private meditation upon the Scriptures. The whole method of praying was being reshaped. It is here that Anselm was most an innovator, though it is here also that he was closest to the masters before and after him. There is no analysis in Anselm of how to pray—that was left for the Cistercians and the Victorines. But Anselm did give a paragraph indicating how he expected his meditations to be used, and this directive is startling enough in its mixture of prayer with meditation and reading.

Meditation in the strict sense was learning the psalms or other parts of the Scriptures by heart so that they became part of the one praying and issued in prayer. It was the material that set the pace and shaped the meditation. For Anselm, the emphasis is not on the material used but on the person praying. He uses these things— place, time, the subject matter—in whatever way helps him to pray; they are arranged so that the reader can choose parts, and leave out parts, so that he can "ponder more deeply those things that make him want to pray." It was a deliberate withdrawal from external things for a close, intimate exploration of one's own inner self. It is in this setting no longer enough for prayer to be brief and simple; it is a lengthy examination of oneself rather than of the Scriptures. The starting point is a mental one—a phrase from the Scriptures, a story, a person, a situation—and from it the whole of the person praying comes into a relationship, which in its turn leads to the thresholds of prayer. Here there is scope for sighs, groans, tears;

emotion as well as intellect is being deliberately used to make the whole of oneself become alert to pray. *Affectus* as a way of prayer had been given a new and dramatic meaning.

The older tradition had nothing like that. To pray had meant to say the psalter; to meditate was to learn the Scriptures. Moments of personal encounter or illumination were expressed briefly, if at all. The "new" prayer has a great deal to do with a profound change at that time in the ways of self-expression and self-understanding—a major change of sentiment in the history of mankind which formed the key-note of the twelfth century. These were the prayers that were now wanted and appreciated. Anselm was asked to provide them. They circulated widely during his lifetime, and very rapidly received that most significant form of flattery—imitation. The prayers, and those based on them, have so formed the devotional temper of medieval Europe that one can hardly imagine how anyone prayed without them.

The development was not all gain; even in Anselm there is a vein of sheer sentimentality which was to be imitated by lesser men with dire results. Moreover, in other hands his style could be tedious; it is not everyone who can write our prayers for us. But Anselm shaped devotion into the channels of meditation on the humanity of Christ, on his mother, and on personal confrontation with the mysteries of the Christian faith, in an appeal to emotion, intellect, and will in a new way. The proper end of this vein of devotion lies in the great devotional poetry of the late Middle Ages. The hymn by a Cistercian, *Jesu dulcis memoria*, takes up the theme of Anselm's first meditation; the *Stabat Mater* derives from his "Prayer to Christ'; and the great rolling periods of the *Dies Irae* are in direct line with the third and the first of his meditations.

VI

Another deeply Christian theme, that of the unity of souls in the love of God, was also vital to Anselm's understanding of prayer. When Hugh the Hermit asked him for help about prayer, he referred to his own comments in the last chapters of the *Proslogion* about the unity of souls in love in the perfection of the vision of God as the most essential way of entering into prayer with God, with the saints and with men, adding the phrase that best sums up his approach to prayer: "Give love . . . and receive the kingdom; love and possess."[196] This love of the brethren was another monastic concept that formed Anselm's prayers. He prayed within a lifelong commitment to God with others who had also chosen each other in God.

Friendship, first with God and the saints and as a result with others, was for Anselm fundamental. The fact that this friendship extended outside the monastery to others who, like the Countess Matilda, Queen Mathilda, and the Princess Adelaide, were secular women seriously committed to conversion of life and to prayer is another mark of the expanding mood of the times. The influential doctrine of friendship, later so closely associated with the Cistercians, was present in embryo in Anselm, especially in his early letters and in the *Prayers*. Always practical and realistic, Anselm prayed from his own experience of friendship and therefore first for his own personal friends, those whom "your love has impressed more clearly upon my heart."[197] This was the place to start, but his theological understanding of love led him to see that friendship was not restricted to those he knew personally; he called those "friends" all who were joined to him by monastic or Christian profession; and he prayed that any who hated him would also be his friends one day. In the prayers that are addressed to the saints,

---

196 Anselm, Letter 112 to Hugh the Hermit, *The Letters of Anselm of Canterbury,* trans. Walter Frohlich, 3 vols. (Kalamazoo, MI, 1990), vol. 1, pp. 268–71.

197 *Prayers and Meditations,* 18. Prayer for Friends, l. 44, p. 213.

he appealed to their friendship, as powerful friends of God—in the Prayer to St. John the Evangelist this is the dominant theme: the love of John for Christ, of Christ for John, and the place of the one who prays within that circle of friendship.[198] In the *Proslogion* it is friendship that is the unchanging bond in heaven: "they will love God more than themselves, and each other as themselves."[199]

This bond of friendship had for Anselm its origin and end in love of *"dulcis et benignus Dominus Jesus Christus."* He saw all love as based on the friendship between man and God. It was to be fully realised in the unbroken circle of love in heaven, but on earth the monastery should be a school of love, a *schola Christi,* a claustral paradise opening onto heaven. In his letter to Hugh the Hermit, this sense of the companionship of the saints is offered as the basis of prayer for the hermit as much as for the coenobite. The stress on solitude and individual withdrawal in the Anselmian method was not the definition of the self in opposition to others but the self always seen as part of the body of Christ and within the presence of "a great cloud of witnesses" (Heb. 12:1). The servant whom the child had seen with the Lord in heaven was always present to the man of prayer.

Bernard of Clairvaux once said, "Give me a soul who loves God alone and everything for his sake";[200] he would have found that soul perfectly in Anselm. But for Anselm, as for Bernard, the contrite contemplation of Jesus was not the end of prayer. The end was the piercing of the heart by joy in the vision of God. This longing desire for heaven concluded each of the *Prayers,* and came to its finest expression at the end of the *Proslogion*: after a meditation on the unity of eternal love in heaven in the vision of God, Anselm prayed,

---

198 *Prayers and Meditations,* 12. Prayer to St. John the Evangelist (2), pp. 163–71.
199 *Proslogion,* cap. 25, in *Prayers and Meditations,* ll. 687–88, p. 263.
200 Bernard of Clairvaux, *Sermons on the Song of Songs,* 15:5.

Let your love grow in me here
and there let it be fulfilled,
so that here my joy may be in great hope,
and there in full reality . . .
Let my whole being desire it
until I enter into the joy of my Lord,
who is God one and triune blessed forever. Amen.[201]

Anselm, then, prayed out of an assured monastic theology, as part of a tradition of prayer, but also as one of the creators of the new age. It is, of course, impossible to tell how influential his prayers were for the personal devotion of those to whom he gave them, but it is clear his prayers were widely known and used. They were imitated in writing during his lifetime by the monks Elmer of Canterbury and Ralph of Battle and by others later. Thomas Becket had a copy of Anselm's prayers, and there is a continuous manuscript tradition of the prayers from the twelfth century onwards. In the use made of them, there is no doubt that the original words were changed. Though later prayers in this style changed the careful balance of thought and emotion of Anselm's genuine works, the possibility of such changes were part of Anselm's aim: the prayers were his own meditations, and the only point in sharing them was that they might help others to find their own voice for prayer.

Anselm never taught prayer: he was known as someone who prayed. He prayed for his friends and let them see how he did it, and when he died in Canterbury in Holy Week 1109, he had ensured the continuation of the traditions of Christian prayer, revitalised, into a new age. To the end of his life he prayed, "God of truth, I ask that I may receive that my joy may be full." His search for God was never joyless, and it was never static; he stretched his emotions as well as his mind to the utmost in order to come to that "fullness of joy" which is true humanity.

201 *Proslogion*, cap. 26, in *Prayers and Meditations*, ll. 771–74, 795–97, pp. 266–67.

Perhaps it is especially relevant today to return to Anselm's genuine prayers, when in academic circles the concept of God has been so rarefied that he can seem not only irrelevant but non-existent, and when among the devout attention to the humanity of Jesus has dissolved into personal sentimentality, and to remember how thought and emotion were uniquely united in Anselm as faith seeking understanding in both his thought and his prayer. It seems to me that Anselm is an example of prayer for the third millennium; he has been continually used in this way during previous centuries and his work adapted according to the needs of each; now is the moment to return to the authentic prayers of Anselm himself and learn from him again how to pray today. His life of prayer was seen in his own times as a reality, a sincere approach to God, and it was this that drew people to him, and it is that which makes him still a man of prayer for a new age: "These works show us," wrote Durandus, "your devoted tears . . . and bring forth ours . . . a stream runs from your heart into our heart."[202] Or, as Anselm wrote himself, "Give love and receive the kingdom; love and possess."[203]

SUGGESTIONS FOR FURTHER READING

Eadmer. *Life of St Anselm*. Edited and translated by R. W. Southern. Oxford, 1972.

Evans, G. R. *Anselm*. London, 1989.

The Prayers and Meditations of Saint Anselm, with the Proslogion, Translated by Benedicta Ward, SLG. Penguin Classics, 1973. Third impression 2002.

Southern, R. W. *St Anselm and His Biographer*. Cambridge, 1963. Re-issued as *Anselm, a Portrait in a Landscape*. Cambridge, 1990.

202 Letter 70, from Durandus, abbot of La Chaise-Dieu, to Anselm, *Letters*, vol. 1, p. 193.
203 Letter 112, to Hugh the Hermit, *Letters*, vol. 1, p. 269.

6

TWELFTH-CENTURY
ENGLISH HERMITS

✦ ■ ✦ ■ ✦ ■ ✦ ■ ✦ ■ ✦ ■ ✦ ■ ✦

I n the second half of the eleventh century, Peter Damian, the Prior
of Fonte Avellana, wrote about a problem recently raised in his
community: "Many of the brethren, followers of the eremitic life,
have asked me whether, since they live alone in their cells, it is right for
them to say *Dominus vobiscum, Jube, domine, benedicere,* and the like,
despite the fact that they are alone." He goes on to answer the question
himself with a long letter on the hermit life which is known as "The
Book of the Lord Be with You,"[204] in which he included the following
passage as the kernel of his argument:

> He [the hermit] sees as present with the eyes of the spirit all
> those for whom he prays . . . he knows that all who are praying
> with him are present in spiritual communion. . . . Therefore
> let no brother who lives alone in a cell be afraid to utter words
> which are common to the whole Church, for although he is
> separated by space from the congregation of the faithful, yet he
> is bound together with them all by love in the unity of the faith;
> although they are absent in the flesh, they are near at hand in the
> mystical unity of the Church.[205]

204 Peter Damian, "The Book of the Lord Be with You," trans. Patricia McNulty, in
    Peter Damian, Selected Writings (London: Faber, 1959), pp. 53–54.
205 Ibid., pp. 73–74.

In examining the exact ways in which hermits were connected with communities in external matters, it is essential to have in mind that these external links are meant to subserve and express that deep inner unity in which the hermit is "bound together with them all by love in the unity of the faith." When a monk goes to live apart from his brothers, it is possible to note and mark the ways in which he is separate from them, but what cannot be assessed in terms of legislation is the main part of his life which is concerned with affirming his unity in Christ with them all; in the mysterious words of St. Antony, the father of hermits, "my life is with my neighbour."[206]

On the level of external contact between hermits and society, however, this fundamental spiritual link has been expressed in different ways in different ages. I would like to examine here the tradition within monasticism in the West in the Middle Ages, with special reference to some developments in the twelfth century. The material is taken mostly from the lives of saints, but I have also tried to show how the relationship between hermits and society was viewed in theory as well as in practice.

The Rule of St. Benedict was the basis of Christian monasticism from the eighth century to the eleventh. It is often supposed that this Rule formally excluded the idea of the hermit life, and a superficial reading of the text alone supports this claim. However, no Rule can be assessed truly simply by its written words, and there is ample evidence that hermits continued to exist within the Benedictine tradition, and to find their justification within the Rule itself. Cassiodorus, like Jerome and Cassian, had seen the hermit life as a stage within the monastic life, and at Vivarium he provided hermitages for this purpose;[207] it appeared to the early Benedictines that this was the teaching also of the Rule of

---

206 Cf. *The Sayings of the Desert Fathers*, trans. Benedicta Ward, SLG (Mowbray, 1975), Anthony 9, p. 3.
207 Cassiodorus, *Institutiones*, ed. R. A. B. Mynors (Oxford, 1937), p. 74.

St. Benedict. In the first chapter of the Rule, four kinds of monks are discussed, and though the Rule provides most of all for the "strong race of coenobites,"[208] the hermits are described as the end product of the coenobitic life:

> After long probation in the monastery, having learnt in association with many brethren how to fight against the devil, [they] go out well-armed from the ranks of the community to the solitary combat of the desert. They are now able to live without the help of others, and by their own strength and God's assistance to fight against the temptations of mind and body.[209]

The monastery is "a school of the Lord's service"[210] in which men attain "some degree of virtue and the rudiments of monastic observance"[211]; but the Rule claims only to be "a little Rule for beginners."[212] For those who "hasten to the perfection of the monastic life," St. Benedict recommends "the teaching of the holy Fathers . . . the Conferences of Cassian, and his Institutes, and the Lives of the Fathers and also the Rule of our holy father, Basil."[213] St. Benedict himself lived as a hermit, and it is probable that at Monte Cassino there were, as at Vivarium, separate cells for hermits. In the following centuries it is clear that there were hermits attached to monastic houses as a matter of course, and, though the perils of such a life and its rarity were increasingly recognized, there is constant evidence of its existence. Grimlaic in his *Rule for Solitaries* in the ninth century says, "To enter the solitary life is the highest perfection; to live imperfectly in solitude is to incur the greatest damnation."[214]

208 *Rule of St Benedict*, ed. and trans. J. McCann, p. 16.
209 Ibid., chap. 1, p. 14.
210 Ibid., Prologue, p. 12.
211 Ibid., chap. 73, p. 160.
212 Ibid., p. 162.
213 Ibid., p. 160.
214 Grimlaic, *Regula Solitarium*, cap. 23, PL 103, col. 604.

Archaeological discoveries have given evidence of hermitages around monasteries, and particularly near Cluny, which was as much a centre for hermit life as for liturgical devotion.[215] Many chroniclers describe hermits, and the fact of their existence is apparent from many saints' lives. Conciliar decrees and monastic customaries tried to exercise some control over the entry of monks into such a life and over their subsequent activities. These hermits had been monks and, after living in a monastery for some time, they went, with the blessing of their abbot, to live alone or with one or two companions. Their lives are described in terms familiar from the fourth century and the beginnings of monasticism; solitude, prayer, ascetic practices, and simplicity of life were their characteristics.

In the reasons for their choice of such a life, and in the paths that led them there, they differed widely. There was, for instance, Wulsi of Evesham, a layman who was professed at Crowland in the eleventh century, and who found himself unable to participate in the liturgical and administrative life of a large community; he became a hermit in a cave near Evesham. On the other hand, Maurus, a former abbot of Fulda, chose to enter the eremitical life because he would have leisure there for study.[216] There were monks trained in the East who settled as hermits in the midst of the Western coenobitic communities—for instance, Symeon of Trier and Constantine of Malmesbury, and both were accepted and praised. There were hermits who received the blessing of their abbot to embrace a life of solitude permanently; there were also part-time hermits. Notably, there were bishops and abbots, busy administrators, who had cells to which they could retire. Hermedland, first abbot of Aindre, always

---

215 I am greatly indebted for information about Cluny, and about the hermit movements as a whole, to an unpublished thesis by Henrietta Leyser, "The New Eremitical Movements in Western Europe, 1000–1150" (Oxford, 1966).

216 Rudolph, *Miracula sanctorum in Fuldenses ecclesias translatorum, Monumenta Germaniae Historica, Scriptores*, XV, i, p. 340.

spent Lent in solitude and at the end of his life retired permanently to a hermitage.[217]

There was a peaceful relationship of concord between these hermits and their communities. At times a hermit might be recalled because of the needs of his house, most of all if he were needed as abbot for a time. Monks would visit their hermits and consult them on spiritual matters, and some of the hermits found it proper to their vocation to return to the monastery for the liturgy on Sundays and feast days. Hermits were relatively few, and it was because the numbers remained small that this peaceful coexistence was possible. Customaries sometimes legislated for a percentage of hermits being out of community at any one time, and this was never more than 10 percent. In all this the tradition both of the West and of the East does not seem to diverge: the hermit was a monk who sought solitude for a longer or shorter time, who maintained links with the monastery in certain ways, and who was allowed for the rest to follow out his vocation as an individual, however God called him. With the twelfth century there is a change, and this is closely connected with what is often called the "crisis of coenobitism" in the West.

It is clear that in the twelfth century a new type of hermit emerged. The traditional pattern of a monk who entered the hermit life after training in the monastery was still recognized on the same terms as before, but there were many also who had either never been monks or who had found the monastic life in some way unacceptable. With these new hermits a distinction was made between monks and hermits along sharper and less amicable lines. The problems involved were complex and to some extent meant that the term *hermit* and also the term *monk* were being redefined. Since the influence of this is still with us, especially in our concepts of contemplative communities, a closer look at this movement is essential.

217 *Vita S. Hermelandi abb. Antrens, Acta Sanctorum Ordinis S. Benedicti,* ed. Mabillon, III, i, p. 396.

There were, first, those who began the hermit life without monastic training. Then there were those who had been monks but had undertaken a hermit way of life more or less as a clearing-ground until a concept of community again emerged for them. In the first group there were three famous English hermits: Wulfric of Haslebury, Christina of Markyate, and Godric of Finchale. All of them began their hermit lives outside the monastic structures, though all of them developed close relationships with communities later.

Wulfric was born of a middle-class English family in the reign of William Rufus at Compton Martin in Somerset. He was ordained below the canonical age and lived as a careless and worldly cleric at Deverill near Warminster, where he neglected his duties for hunting. In about 1125 he underwent a conversion, and was also offered the cure of the village where he had been born. There, under the protection of William Fitzwalter, he became an anchorite in a cell in the wall of the church, where he lived until his death. The villagers supported him and turned to him for spiritual advice, and possibly for practical help, since it seems at least possible to deduce from his life that his cell was used as a kind of strong room in which villagers could safely leave their money in the troubled times of King Stephen. Wulfric was known to St. Bernard by repute and was approved by him. He was consulted by kings and lords as well as local people, and he had some connection with both the local Cluniac priory of Montecute and the Cistercian house at Ford. The monks of Montecute tried to claim his body after his death, but he was in fact buried in his cell. John, a monk of Ford, wrote his life with admiration and affection. [218]

Like Wulfric, Christina of Markyate did not enter a novitiate in a religious house. This may well have been because she had literally no chance to do so. The opposition of her parents, lack of a dowry,

218 John of Ford, *Life of Wulfric of Haslebury,* ed. Dom Maurice Bell, Somerset
Record Society, vol. XLVII, 1933.

and the prohibition of her doing so by the bishop debarred her from any monastic house whatever. In order to fulfil her desire for a life of consecrated virginity, she ran away from home and lived among a close network of hermits who inhabited the district around St. Albans. She joined at first a woman recluse, Alfwen, a hermitess at Flamstead; after two years she went to live with the hermit Roger at Markyate. Roger was one of a remarkable group of hermits who lived near the Abbey of St. Albans, and from them Christina received her training as a hermit. After Roger's death she continued, after a year elsewhere, at Markyate and soon made contact with Geoffrey, the abbot of St. Albans. Roger had been a monk of St. Albans, and Christina's connections with the monastery were close; it seems almost certain that the St. Albans psalter was written at St. Albans for her use. Her friendship with Abbot Geoffrey was deep and continuous, and she was regarded by the other monks as a spiritual guide. It is, however, notable that she did not make her profession as a nun until 1131, after living for many years as a hermit and after being offered the abbatial office at St. Clements, York. Her profession, moreover, was made in the monastery at St. Albans. Women joined her at Markyate, and though the account of her life breaks off before the death of Geoffrey, it is clear that she continued as a recognized and able abbess for the rest of her life. [219]

Godric of Finchale was an English merchant and sailor who converted to a more serious Christianity in Jerusalem. He visited Rome, Compostela, and Jerusalem, and finally returned to his native Northumbria, where he simply went and lived in solitude. Some land at Finchale was leased to him by the bishop of Durham, and he also made contact on a spiritual level with the Durham monks. After some years he decided to place himself under obedience to the prior of Durham, and a more definite relationship with the community emerged. The prior

219 *Christina of Markyate*, ed. and trans. C. Talbot (Oxford, 1959).

sent a monk to say Mass at the hermitage every feast day, and Reginald, Godric's biographer, a monk of Durham, visited him at those times and also was with him when he became ill at the end of his life. A priory of Durham was established eventually at Finchale. [220]

These hermits were part of a new eremitic pattern, and a more famous one of the same kind shows how this solitude could emerge into a new form of community. Stephen of Muret learned about monastic life while visiting the monks of Calabria, but he did not become a monk in any formal sense. Instead, he went alone to a mountain near Muret and there professed himself. [221] His biographer says:

> He had a ring with which he espoused himself to Christ, saying:
> 'I, Stephen, renounce the devil and all his pomps, and devote
> myself to God, Father, Son and Holy Spirit, God Three and One,
> Living and True'. He also wrote out this formula and placed it on
> his head saying: 'I, Stephen, promise to serve God in this desert
> in the Catholic faith, and for this cause I place this form upon
> my head and this ring on my finger that at the day of my death
> it may be unto me according to my promise. . . . I ask you, Lord,
> to restore to me the wedding garment and count me among the
> sons of the Church at the wedding feast of your Son.'[222]

Other solitaries joined Stephen, and the Order of Grandmont was formed. The Grandmontines kept the eremitic life as their basic aim; all the administration was in the hands of the *conversi,* and a standard of evangelical poverty was maintained which foreshadowed that of the Franciscans later. They claimed to follow only the Gospel and not even the Fathers. Their solitude, however, was like that which evolved for other hermits, a corporate solitude, in which each member of the group

---

220 Reginald of Durham, *Libellus de vita et miraculis S. Godrici,* ed. J. Stevenson, Surtees Society XX (1845).
221 *Vita S. Stephani confessoris (Muretensis),* PL 204, cols. 1013ff.
222 Ibid., col. 1016.

lived in varying degrees of personal solitude; but the characteristic feature of them as a group was that they were apart from society.

These four did not pass through any formal novitiate, nor was their link with the older monastic communities that of formal training and profession. The hermit life was not for them the final stage of a monastic vocation in which they were living out their monastic life under different conditions, but basically still as an integral part of their community. They are typical of the new understanding of hermit life in the twelfth century. Stephen of Grandmont provides a link between this kind of new hermit and the more famous kind who were hermit-founders. The new monastic orders of Camaldoli, Chartreuse, Savigny, Fontevrault, and above all, Cîteaux, were the end product of the hermit explosion of the early years of the twelfth century. Besides these, more than fifty other communities which adopted a communal rule of life began from hermit foundations. For instance, there was a group of hermits at Llanthony early in the twelfth century, and by 1120 they had become a house of canons following the Rule of St. Augustine, with customs from Aldgate, Colchester, and Merton.[223] Besides these, many houses of hermits became affiliated to Cîteaux, including Morimond and Pontigny.

The founders of these communities lived at first as hermits. Romuald, the founder, with Ludolph and Julian, of Fonte Avellana, first of all tried to persuade his community at St. Apollinaris in Classe to adopt his ideas, then left it to live alone until a new community formed around him.[224] John Gualbert lived as a hermit at Vallombrosa, and the monastery that grew there continued to be known as the Hermitage, both because of its austerity and its remoteness from the world. Stephen of Obazine, Bruno of Cologne, and Vitalis of Savigny all contemplated a form of solitude which was not that of existing communities. Two things distinguished their idea of hermit life from that of the more traditional hermits: first,

223 J. Dickinson, *The Origins of the Austin Canons* (London: SPCK, 1950), pp. 111–12.
224 Peter Damian, *Vita Romualdi,* PL 144, col. 336.

their concept of corporate solitude; and secondly, their desire for stability and obedience to recognized authority among themselves. The idea of solitude in a group is different from the idea of personal solitude. St. Norbert said, like any hermit in any age, "I do not want to stay in the towns; I prefer places that are deserted and uncultivated."[225] But he did not expect to stay in the desert alone. Vitalis of Savigny withdrew to the "desert," but it was in company with other recluses.[226] The desire for obedience was a corporate ideal, and when combined with the new concept of solitude as being simply away from the towns, led to the evolution of hermits into communities.

Of the new communities, Camaldoli, Chartreuse, Fonte Avellana, and Grandmont came closest to the Eastern concept of a lavra, though with more monks than was usual in the East. The brothers lived in separate cells, and the degree of communal life was minimal. At Fonte Avellana, for instance, they met only on Sundays for Mass and Office, while at the Grande Chartreuse they only sang the Office of Vigils together. At Grandmont the separation of the group as a whole from the rest of the world included a stress upon absolute individual solitude as well. The monks in these groups were called hermits. It was not envisaged that they would move on to a greater personal solitude; it was a corporate life in which it was held that the hermit ideal was already realized. It is possible to see this kind of group as a restoration, almost certainly an unconscious restoration, of the idea of the skete which had fallen out of use in the West; whereas the Eastern skete was a stage towards the complete hermit life, the hermits of Camaldoli and Chartreuse were basically committed to their monastery.

225 Herman, *Liber III de miraculis S. Mariae Laudenensis*, chap. 3, *Monumenta Germaniae Historica, Scriptores*, XII, p. 656.
226 Ordericus Vitalis, *Historia Ecclesiastica*, Bk. VIII, chap. 27, ed. A. le Prévost and L. Delisle, (Paris, 1838–1855), p. 449.

The most famous of these new communities was, of course, Cîteaux, and the differences between the old and new forms of monastic life received dramatic publicity as a conflict between the Cluniacs and Cistercians. The latter were, more than any of the new orders, concerned to integrate solitude into community. They began as a group of hermits and called their new home a "desert"; hermits individually and in groups were to join them later. But the Cistercian way of life was basically inimical to the concept of individual solitude. The Order of Cîteaux claimed to have found the "more perfect way" of St. Benedict's Rule and to have embodied it in their corporate life. This idea of integrated solitude could cause difficulty when members joined who discovered a desire in themselves for the traditional hermit withdrawal; it was seen as a reproach, as opting out of what all wanted and had, and in this it is possible to see the problems that later faced contemplative communities whose members sought greater solitude from a context which *de facto* claimed to have it already.

The hermits formed communities, and with this they posed a new question about the meaning of the term *hermit*. The topic gave ample scope to the twelfth century's attrait for categorisation, but in discussions of the matter the hermit escaped too rigid a definition in a significant way. The *Libellus de Ordinibus Diversis,* for instance, lays the stress in differentiating between monk and hermit on the life itself: "I do not argue much about the name when I see the works performed . . . without the life the name alone is empty."[227] In this treatise the term *hermit* is extended to include the new hermit communities. The monk, the writer says, is a hermit when he goes into the desert with like-minded men:

He will penetrate the innermost part of the desert with Antony where he will merit the aid of the angels against the demons and

227 *Libellus de Ordinibus Diversis,* ed. Constable and Smith (Oxford, 1972), p. 26.

the company of good men following him for God's sake; when you have done well you must go out into the mountain with Jesus and pass the night there in prayer.[228]

It seems that by the end of the twelfth century the hermit was beginning to be defined as "ascetic" rather than as one who lives alone. The most extreme example I know of this redefinition is in the accounts of the martyrdom of Archbishop Thomas Becket at Canterbury. When the monks stripped the dead body of this man who had not in life been notable for solitude, either corporate or personal, they discovered that he had worn a hair shirt. "Lo," they exclaimed, "here indeed was a true monk *and hermit*."[229]

The evidence of the hermit movements in the West in the twelfth century points to several conclusions. First, there is the overall tendency to understand the hermit life as no longer exclusively the summit of monastic life in community. Two aspects of this view have their bearing on contemporary approaches to eremitism in the Church. There were, first of all, those who saw the hermit life as a preliminary to life in community; from this view there emerges a new understanding of the relationship between community and solitary, in which the stress is placed upon the solitude of the group rather than the individual. It is from these groups who tried to embody the ideals of solitude within communities that the modern "contemplative" communities derive, in at least certain aspects. The problems posed for these communities with regard to the individual hermit remain.

Secondly, in the twelfth century it is known that there were hermits who had never undergone any religious training in a community and whose relationship with the monks was not necessarily of a formal nature. This underlines the essentially free and unstructured nature of

228   Ibid.
229   *Materials for the History of Archbishop Thomas Becket*, ed. J. C. Robertson, Rolls Series, 1875–1833, vol. I, 12; emphasis added.

the hermit vocation, which emphasizes the fact that there will always be in the Church those whom God calls into the wilderness and keeps there for their love of the Crucified to overflow in ways of prayer. That is the service Peter Damian speaks of in the quotation with which this chapter began. It is then for the monks and for the Church to enable them to remain hidden within the quiver of his love.

7
FAITH SEEKING UNDERSTANDING
Anselm of Canterbury *and* Julian of Norwich

✦ ▪ ✦ ▪ ✦ ▪ ✦ ▪ ✦ ▪ ✦ ▪ ✦ ▪ ✦

At first sight Anselm of Canterbury and Julian of Norwich seem to have little in common. The one, a monk from Normandy who became archbishop of Canterbury under William Rufus, was one of the greatest of medieval scholars, writing his prayers and meditations in beautiful, highly wrought Latin in the eleventh century. The other, an unlettered laywoman and a recluse in the town of Norwich, wrote (or perhaps dictated) her revelations and meditations on them in English in the fourteenth century. Both composed a short devotional work, however: Julian the *Revelations of Divine Love* and Anselm *The Prayers and Meditations*. It seems clear from these that they both belong to the same tradition of Christian prayer.

In comparing them it is not suggested that there is any actual dependence, for two reasons: first that Julian would not have been able to read the Latin prayers if they had been available to her; and second that as a clearly defined body of work the *Prayers* were not available to anyone before the twentieth century. This is because within a few years of Anselm's death the original prayers were surrounded by a host of prayers in the same vein by other writers, all of which were attributed to him. It is only in the past fifty years that the genuine *Prayers and Meditations* have again been distinguished in the form in which Anselm meant them to be used, and it is only now that Anselm's teaching as an ascetical theologian can really be appreciated. The body of Anselm's prayers was not available to Julian, but there can be no doubt that she was influenced by the ethos that he had been so largely responsible for creating, and that there are very significant similarities between them. It is of more interest for us to see the same methods, the same approaches, the same understanding in two such dissimilar people, than to attempt any more academic discussion of them. It may be, who knows, that the tradition they both used can be of real significance for us in our same desire for God.

In the first place Anselm and Julian are both people who can truly be called theologians, in the sense of the theologian as one whose prayer is true. Anselm was pre-eminently a theologian, formed by the undivided tradition of Christian doctrine, and bending all the powers of his mind to understanding that faith. This total acceptance of Christian dogma was equally present in Julian, as she says, "I shall always believe what is held, preached and taught by Holy Church . . . it was with this well in mind that I looked at the revelation so diligently" (*Revelations,* chap. 9). In his greatest philosophical work, which is also the greatest of his meditations, Anselm approaches his search for God in the same way: "I desire to understand a little of your love, which my heart already believes and loves . . . unless I believe I shall not understand" (*Proslogion,* chap. 1).[230] The original title Anselm gave to the *Proslogion* was in fact "Faith Seeking Understanding," a phrase which sums up his whole approach to theology and prayer, and is as true of Julian as of him.

In both of them there is this complete unity of belief and understanding, the mind at the service of the heart, which makes them truly Christian scholars. To accept the truths of the faith was for them

---

230 Quotations from St. Anselm are taken from *The Prayers and Meditations of St Anselm,* translated by Benedicta Ward, SLG (London: Penguin Classics, 1973).

a liberation, not a restriction. No one could accuse either of them of being simply echoes of other men's ideas: in both there is originality and personal insight to an astonishing degree. It is to be expected, perhaps, that Julian, whose book-learning was limited, should not have quoted other writers very often; but that Anselm, one of the most learned men of his, or any age, quoted equally infrequently is more surprising. The Bible, of course, permeated their thought and writings, but even there they rarely quote. They have, it seems, so absorbed and made their own the revelation of God in Christ that they were free to speak for that revelation in terms of their own personality and understanding.

The idea of "faith *seeking* understanding" is another concept that they have in common—the mobile, flexible, developing nature of faith lies behind their works. Julian reflected for thirty years on the meaning of her revelations, making an interior journey ever deeper into "the Lord's meaning." Anselm taught that knowledge of God is a reaching forward and a continuing inner journey: "Come now, little man, stir up your torpid mind . . . flee a while from your occupations . . . enter into the inner chamber of your mind . . . close the door and seek Him" (*Proslogion,* chap. 1). This inner world of movement and discovery demands for its proper realisation, however, a measure of withdrawal, of solitude, of stillness. It is essentially an interior adventure, made by Anselm in the "inner chamber," and by Julian in her anchoress's cell.

Firmly based in theological truth, both Anselm and Julian prepared to "seek understanding" in solitude, and they sought it by paths that are very similar. In both of them there are stages of spiritual progress, stages which were to be most clearly described by St. Bernard. At the beginning of the *Revelations* Julian says: "Through the grace of God and the teaching of Holy Church, I developed a strong desire to receive three wounds, namely, the wound of contrition, the wound of genuine compassion, and the wound of sincere longing for God" (*Revelations,* chap. 2). This threefold pattern of prayer is the same in the teaching of Anselm. It has, of course, a long history in the spirituality of both East and West, but at the end of the eleventh century Anselm articulated it for the West in a new way. Against the background of a liturgically centred tradition of prayer, he set out a way of personal, interior prayer focussed in the pattern of three wounds, or piercings, of the soul by God. The first wound was that of contrition, true sorrow for sin, and self-abasement; the second wound was that of compassion, known through the sufferings of Christ; and the third wound was that of longing desire for God. These three wounds were to pierce and break the hard heart so that God's work of prayer could really begin. In each of the prayers this pattern is followed. It is not a once-for-all way, in which one stage is finally left behind and then another undertaken; rather it is a continual pattern of prayer, into which one enters more deeply all the time.

The first wound that Anselm sets at the beginning of all his prayers is that of sorrow for sin, and he uses every verbal means to bring this home to himself: "I am afraid of my life; for when I examine myself closely, it seems to me that my whole life is either sinful or sterile" (Med. 1). "Alas for my wretched state, how my sins cry out against me . . . immoderate offence, offence against my God" (Prayer to St. John the Evangelist, 1). "The Judge Himself is my stern accuser and I am clearly a sinner against Him" (Prayer to St. Paul). In Julian there is the same awareness of sin: "Sin is the sharpest scourge"; "holy Church shall be shaken at the world's sorrow, anguish, and tribulation" (*Revelations,* chap. 28); "the shame that our foul deeds caused" (*Revelations,* chap. 77).

This awareness of sin and self-abasement is not, in either Anselm or Julian, a matter of psychological or personal guilt; it is rather a deep theological awareness of the infinite glory of God, and of the contrast of the horror of any sin which offends against it. "How can you call any sin small," Anselm asks, "when it is committed against God?" In Julian it is not reflection upon her own misdeeds but the sense of "our foul, black, shameful deeds which hid the fair, splendid and blessed Lord God" that provokes contrition (*Revelations,* chap. 10).

It is in the second wound, however, that the similarity between Anselm and Julian is most marked: this is their "compassion" with the sufferings of Christ. The whole of Julian's writing is based on her immediate and vivid experience of the passion of Christ: "I had," she says, "some experience of the passion of Christ, but by his grace I wanted still more. I wanted actually to be there with Mary Magdalene and the others who loved him. . . . I would be one of them and suffer with him" (*Revelations,* chap. 2). This is Anselm's approach in his Prayer to Christ, an imaginative consideration of the details of the sufferings of Christ which found its ultimate term many years later in the emotions of the Stabat Mater. In the Prayer to Christ he asks: "Why, O my soul, were you not there to be pierced by the sword of bitter sorrow. . . . Why did you not see the nails violate the hands and feet of your Creator? Would that I with happy Joseph might have taken down my Lord from the cross, wrapped him in spiced grave-clothes, and laid him in the tomb." This desire to experience personally the human side of the sufferings of Christ and of his mother received new impetus from Anselm and coloured the prayers and the art of the later Middle Ages as, incidentally, did his understanding of the tenderness of the child of Bethlehem and his mother. The "homely," as Julian would say, was seen as an integral part of the "holy."

The third "piercing" for both Anselm and Julian is that of longing desire for the joys of the vision of God. In both writers this theme counterbalances their emphasis on sin, pain, and estrangement.

In Anselm each prayer ends with a passage full of longing for God
and the bliss of heaven: "He fell asleep in the Lord," he says of St.
Stephen, "happy man, to rest in joy and joy in rest; safe home, you
are filled with glory, your joy does not change, your light does not
fail. . . . O rich and blessed peace, how far I am from you; alas for
my unhappiness, where I am not, where I am, and, alas, I know not
where I shall be." This theme of the longing of the exiled soul for God
lies at the heart of Anselm's understanding of prayer, our restoration
to the image of God. This is a fundamental monastic theme in any
age which goes with a great longing and a great and positive joy. In
Julian there is always this longing for God, and there is also a great
deal about joy. It is the joy of God which she sees most of all, his
joy in his work of redemption and our joyful response to that work
in delight and thankfulness: "When we are done with grief, our
eyes will suddenly be enlightened" (*Revelations,* chap. 83); "we shall
partake of God's blessedness forever, praising him and thanking him"
(*Revelations,* chap. 85).

One further similarity of these writers in this connection is that
"this holy marvelling delight in God which is love" is expressed in
terms of the physical senses. For instance, Julian writes: "We shall
see him truly and feel him fully, hear him spiritually, smell him
delightfully and taste him sweetly" (*Revelations,* chap. 43). Anselm
frequently uses this sensual imagery, especially about eating or
tasting the sweetness of the word of God, and in the last chapter
of the *Proslogion* he describes the joys of the saints in terms of the
perfect fulfilment of all the senses.

For both Anselm and Julian, the centre and pivot of their approach
to God by the three "piercings" resolves itself into one word—Jesus.
In Anselm's first Meditation, when he has thought with anguish of
the terror of the Last Judgement, he exclaims: "But it is he, it is Jesus

the same is my judge between whose hands I tremble. . . . Jesus, Jesus, be to me for thy name's sake, Jesus." Julian says simply: "I wanted no other heaven but Jesus, who shall be my bliss when I come there" (*Revelations*, chap. 19). The essence of this approach is perhaps found in the Cistercian hymn *Jesu dulcis memoria*—Jesus, the very thought is sweet—but in none of these writers is this concentration on Jesus sentimental or naive. Julian chooses Jesus for her heaven "whom I saw only in pain at that time"; "the strength of your salvation, the cause of your freedom, the price of your redemption . . . through this, and not otherwise than through this, will you remain in Christ and Christ in you, and your joy will be full" (*Revelations*, Med. 3).

This combination of pain and joy, sorrow and bliss, points to the last and perhaps deepest point of similarity between Anselm and Julian. Their ability to see in the details of suffering the truth of glory is brought out in an unusual and striking way in the concept they share of Christ as our mother. This idea of the maternity of God is found in the Old Testament, and in St. Paul, and had found echoes in several medieval writers of the eleventh century; but Anselm gave it a profound and disturbing meaning in his great Prayer to St. Paul. He sees St. Paul as his mother in the faith, and then turns to apply the same terms to Christ: "And you, Jesus, are you not also a mother? It is by your death that we have been born; longing to bear sons into life, you tasted death and by dying you begot them." Christ is seen here as bearing sons by his passion on the cross, a deeper understanding of the meaning of suffering than a simple analogy about the love of Christ being like that of a mother for her children. Anselm sees love as essentially life-giving, not as sentimental or easy. Later in the same prayer he pictures the sinner hiding under the wings of Jesus: "You, my soul, dead in yourself, run under the wings of Jesus your mother, and lament your griefs under his feathers. Ask that your wounds may be healed and that, strengthened, you may live again." This is not the gentleness of a mother with a child, but a fundamental concern with our relationship to Christ and the integral meaning of atonement.

Julian expands this theme in several chapters. "In our mother Christ we grow and develop; in his mercy he reforms and restores us; through his passion, death, and resurrection he has united us to our being" (*Revelations,* chap. 58). And "Jesus is the true mother of our nature for he made us. He is our mother too by grace, because he took our created nature upon himself" (*Revelations,* chap. 59). Both are saying that Christ bore us as his children by his death on the Cross. The pain he suffered was the pain of labour, so that we are his very flesh and blood, and his joy over us is also the cause of all our joy. Moreover, they are making a startlingly modern statement about the nature of God: "Fatherhood, motherhood, and lordship, all in one God," says Julian. "God is both father and mother," according to Anselm. Not that our images of God are of fatherhood or motherhood, but that God himself contains and completes the whole person. Salvation is a new birth of the whole of humanity by the whole God—all humanity is made whole by the whole of God.

Anselm and Julian were three centuries apart in time, and we are more than six hundred years further on again. The gap of general concepts and culture which lies between them and us is wider than in any other century. Yet they represent an unchanging dimension in the relationship between God and the human being who seeks God, from which we can perhaps still learn. They both accepted the objectivity of God as something other than themselves. In order to seek God, they withdrew into solitude and really set themselves to an *ascesis,* a hard labour, to prepare for finding him. They experienced the sense of their own sin before the glory of God; they found mercy through the new life brought to them by Christ on the cross; they learned to rejoice with all their being in Christ and to long for the bliss of his abiding presence in heaven. For them both the final word is the same: love. Julian, in the last chapter of her book, says that after more than fifteen years of meditation on the revelations, it was shown to her that "love was his meaning." Anselm, writing in exile forty years after the composition of the *Prayers*, in his last meditation came to the same conclusion: "Thus have you loved me! Draw me to you, Lord, in the fullness of love. I am wholly yours by creation; make me all yours, too, in love."

8

THREE PREACHERS
Lancelot Andrewes, Jeremy Taylor, Mark Frank

❖ ■ ❖ ■ ❖ ■ ❖ ■ ❖ ■ ❖ ■ ❖ ■ ❖

Lancelot Andrewes (1555–1626)

A burning and a shining candle to all learning and all learned men. . . . A very library to young divines and an oracle to consult at, to laureat and grave divines.[231]

About 4 o'clock in the morning died Lancelot Andrewes, the most worthy bishop of Wincester and the great light of the Christian world.[232]

L
ancelot Andrewes was born at the end of the Marian persecutions in 1555; he lived through the reigns of Elizabeth I and James I, and died early in the reign of Charles I. He was "of honest and religious parents" and went to the Merchant Taylors' School in London. He was at Pembroke College, Cambridge, then a centre of Puritan fervour, and later became Dean of Westminster. He held in turn the Sees of Chichester, Ely, and Winchester, and was court preacher under Elizabeth I and James I. James was said to hold him in great respect and to have asked his advice repeatedly, though he does not seem to have acted upon it.

---

231 John Buckeridge, a sermon preached at Andrewes's funeral, *Works of Lancelot Andrewes*, ed. J. Bliss, 11 vols. (Oxford, 1841–1843), vol. 5, p. 28.
232 Entry in the Diary of Archbishop William Laud, *Works of William Laud*, ed. William Scott (Oxford, 1854), vol. 3, p. 196.

The first thing that comes to mind about Andrewes is his vast scholarship. He knew Greek, Hebrew, Chaldee, Latin, Arabic, Syriac, and fifteen modern languages, of which he learned a new one every year. His most famous and influential work was the *Preces Privatae*, a book of personal devotions which he wrote originally in Greek and Latin. It was said that his Greek prose was in fact even better than his English. "He might," wrote a contemporary, "have served as General Interpreter at the confusion of tongues."[233] As a boy he was quiet and studious, reading rather than playing games, and liking solitary walks. This latter custom continued all his life, and as dean of Westminster the austere master found it a means of making contact with his pupils: "He never walked for his recreation without a brace of small fry, and in that way-faring leisure he had a singular dexterity to fill these narrow vessels with a funnel."[234] All his life he spent each morning in study and simply assumed that others did likewise. "He doubted they were no true scholars who came to speak with him before noon."[235] It was his reputation for erudition that gave him a place at the Hampton Court Conference in 1604 when John Reynolds made his famous request: "May it please your majesty that the Bible be new translated?"[236] Andrewes was in charge of the committee that produced new translations of the books from Genesis to Kings in the Authorized Version of the Bible which was then commissioned.

This unworldly scholar was a friend of King James, "the wisest fool in Christendom," and spent much time at court. He went in and out among the frivolous and grasping courtiers who gathered round the king; he seemed to live in a peculiar atmosphere of holiness. His teaching was largely given in the form of sermons to the court of King James, but some were delivered to a larger audience at St. Paul's

233 Thomas Fuller, *Church History*, vol. IX, p. 126.
234 John Hackett, *Life of John Williams* (1692), p. 45.
235 Henry Isaacson, "Life and Death of Lancelot Andrewes," *Works*, vol. 10, p. xx.
236 William Barlow, *The Summe and Substance of the Conference* (1638), pp. 187–8.

Cross. On Sundays all the London churches finished service early so that the citizens could be present at St. Paul's Cross. These sermons were usually on topical subjects and could be immensely influential. Here Andrewes preached on the Gunpowder Plot and the Gowrie Plot, and to appreciate the harsh, polemical tone of such sermons it is necessary to remember the background against which they were delivered. This was the England which remembered the Armada, the fires of Smithfield, and the massacre of St. Bartholomew as living memories, recent events, and the threats against the Lord's Anointed by Fawkes and Gowrie aroused a rage and hysteria such as can hardly be comprehended in retrospect.

It is in the sermons preached in the more intimate atmosphere of Whitehall that Andrewes's real spiritual power is seen. T. S. Eliot says of these sermons, "He takes each word and derives the world from it, squeezing and squeezing the word until it yields a full juice of meaning which we should never have supposed any word to possess."[237] Each sermon begins with a close analysis of the text, sometimes of each syllable, and every kind of word-play is introduced. The body of the sermon develops these points and applies them to the congregation, very often ending with an invitation to the Eucharist as the fulfilment of the Scriptures. All the word-play and brilliance, all the rhetoric and skill, had one end: to call forth a response from the hearers to the truth of the Scriptures.

The sermons were carefully prepared and worked over; they were delivered from notes and later printed. They are not easy reading, but they contain passages of great beauty and significance. T. S. Eliot used part of a sermon for the Epiphany as the basis of his poem "The Journey of the Magi." The sermon is given here as an example of Andrewes at his best:

237 T. S. Eliot, "For Lancelot Andrewes," *Essays in Style and Order* (London: Faber, 1928), p. 24.

'*Ecce Venerunt*' it is, in the text: and indeed not only the persons, ecce magi, but their very coming deserved an *ecce*. It is an ecce venerunt, theirs, indeed, if we weigh it well, whence they came and whither. Whence? From the East, their own country. Whither? To Jerusalem, that was, to them, a strange land: that was somewhat. They came a long journey, no less than twelve days together. They came an uneasy journey, for their way lay through Arabia Petraea, and the craggy rocks of it. And they came a dangerous journey, through Arabia Deserta, too, and the black 'tents of Kedar' there, then famous for their robberies and even to this day. And they came now, at the worst season of the year. And all, but to do worship at Christ's birth. So great account they made; so highly did they esteem their being at it, as they took all this great travel, and came all this long journey, and came it, at this time. Stayed not their coming, till the opening of the year, till they might have had better weather and way, and have longer days, and so more seasonable and fit to travel in. So desirous were they to come with the first, and to be there, so soon as possibly they might; broke through all these difficulties; *et ecce venerunt*, 'and behold, come they did'.

It is a great passage, but Andrewes did not revel in such descriptions for their own sake—he turns immediately to the application of it to his hearers:

> And we, what excuse shall we have if we come not? If so short and easy a way we come not as from our chambers hither, not to be called a way indeed? Shall not our *Non venerunt* have been an *ecce*, 'Behold, it was stepping but over the threshold, and yet they came not'?
>
> . . . and how shall we do that? I know not any more proper way

left us than to come to that, which Himself by express order hath left us, as the most special remembrance of Himself, to be come to . . . and in the old ritual of the church, we find, that in the cover of the canister, wherein was the sacrament of his Body, there was a star engraven: to shew us, that now the star leads us thither: to His Body, there.

And what shall I say now, but according as St. John saith, and the star, and the wise men say, 'Come'. And He whose star it is, and to whom the wise men came, saith, 'Come'. And let them that are disposed, 'come'. And let whosoever will, take of the 'bread of life which came down from heaven' this day, unto Bethlehem, the house of bread. Of which bread the church is, this day, the house; the true Bethlehem, and all the Bethlehem we have now left to come to, for the bread of life: of that life which we hope for in heaven. And this, our nearest coming, that here we can come, till we shall by another venite come unto Him in his heavenly kingdom. To which he grant us, we may come, that this day came to us in earth, that we thereby might come to Him, and remain with Him forever, Jesus Christ the Righteous.[238]

The fact that his sermons were so often linked with the Eucharist indicates another deep concern of Andrewes: he had a love for the liturgy of the Church of England and a deep reverence for the mystery inherent in worship. About the Eucharist itself he said, "Christ said, this is My Body; not this is My Body in this way," which was echoed in more vivid terms by Taylor when he said, of the Eucharist, "Christ is the food of our souls; this is in a mystery . . . but we are not in

---

238 Andrewes, "Sermon Preached before His Majesty at Whitehall on Monday, 25 December 1620," *Works*, p. 230.

darkness but within the fringes and circles of a bright cloud."[239] This awe and reserve before a great mystery is set out in the *Preces Privatae* in a prayer after communion, a prayer which also shows how deeply Andrewes was versed in the liturgy of Eastern Christendom:

> It is finished and done, so far as in our power, Christ our God, the mystery of thy dispensation; for we have held remembrance of thy death, we have seen the figure of thy resurrection, we have been filled with thy endless life, we have enjoyed thy uncloying dainties of which graciously vouchsafe unto us all to be accounted worthy also in the life to come.[240]

The *Sermons* and the *Preces Privatae* reveal a man of great wisdom and deep devotion who was able to communicate this to others. The penitential tone of the prayers has often been noticed; they are the prayers of a very humble and earnest man, praying out of a real awareness of himself and his condition—with hope and with faith.

'About 4 o'clock in the morning died Lancelot Andrewes . . . the great light of the Christian world', wrote Archbishop Laud in his diary. And a prayer of Bishop Andrewes was answered: 'Abide with me, Lord,' he had prayed, 'for it is towards evening and the day is far spent of this fretful life. Let Thy strength be made perfect in my weakness. Amen.'[241]

---

239 Jeremy Taylor, *The Life of Our Blessed Lord and Saviour Jesus Christ, the Great Exemplar of Sanctity and Holy Life* (hereafter *The Great Exemplar*), *Complete Works*, ed. R. Heber, revised J. Eden (London, 1847), vol. II, p. 514.
240 Lancelot Andrewes, *Preces Privatae*, trans. F. E. Brightman (London, 1903), p. 124.
241 Ibid., p. 107.

Jeremy Taylor (1613–1667)

Let us therefore press after Jesus . . . which is truest religion
and most solemn adoration.[242]

J eremy Taylor has been fortunate both in his biographers and
his critics. Coleridge said he had "more beautiful imagery, more
knowledge of human life and manners, than any prose book in
the language; he has more delicacy and sweetness than any mortal, the
gentle Shakespeare hardly excepted."[243] Hazlitt and Lamb praised him
with equal enthusiasm. His biography was written by a poet, Reginald
Heber, and Sir Edmund Gosse has written of him as a man of letters
and a theologian. His *Holy Living and Holy Dying* holds a unique place
in Christian literature and has enjoyed even more popularity than
Andrewes's *Preces Privatae*.

Taylor was born in 1613. As a young man he attracted the attention
of Archbishop Laud when he preached at St. Paul's in place of a
friend. He held a fellowship at All Souls, Oxford, and was married.
He was chaplain to Charles I at the beginning of the Civil War, was
imprisoned, released at the intervention of the Earl of Carbery, and
then became chaplain at Golden Grove, the Earl's residence in Wales.
There, under the influence of the young and devout Lady Carbery,
he preached most of his sermons and wrote *The Great Exemplar
of Sanctity and Holy Life* and *The Rule and Exercise of Holy Living*.
After the death of Lady Carbery and of his wife, his personal grief
issued in the book *The Rule and Exercise of Holy Dying*. He visited
London during the Protectorate and was friend of the diarist John
Evelyn, but he remained obscure and at times persecuted until the
Restoration. Charles II appointed him bishop of Down and Connor,

242 Jeremy Taylor, *The Great Exemplar*, vol. II, pp. 47–48.
243 S. T. Coleridge, *Notes on the Anglican Divines*, ed. Derwent Coleridge (London,
1853), p. 35.

an appointment which he found not at all to his taste. He died in 1667 at the age of fifty-four.

Taylor was "strong and handsomely proportioned . . . his hair long . . . large dark eyes . . . and an open and intelligent countenance."[244] This open and friendly attitude characterizes his writings.

He has that plain, pragmatic approach to life that is sometimes held to be especially English and Anglican; it is in the tradition of Elizabeth I, Fuller, Hooker, and Cranmer, who would have only "the very pure word of God," that which "may be understood of the people," "that the people may lead quiet and peaceable lives, in all godliness and honesty."[245] Taylor was a scholar, but he did not have the vast erudition of Andrewes, whom he admired. He had an advantage over Andrewes in that by his time the Church of England was further established and no longer needed to argue about its continuity with the early Church. He could write "not like a curious inquirer after new-nothings, but as a pursuer of old truth."[246] He was more concerned with the practical pursuit of holiness than with theological controversy. To Christopher, Lord Hatton, he wrote in the preface to *The Great Exemplar*:

> I am wearied and toiled with rowing up and down in the seas of questions which the interests of Christendom have commenced and in many propositions of which (I am heartily persuaded) I am not certain I am not deceived, but I am most certain that by living in the religion and fear of God, in obedience to the king, in the charities and duties of communion with my spiritual guides, in justice and love with all the world, in their several proportions, I shall not fail of that end which is the perfective of human nature and which will never be obtained by disputing.[247]

244 G. Rust, "A Funeral Sermon," Taylor, *Works*, vol. I, p. cccxxii.
245 Book of Common Prayer, Preface.
246 Taylor, op. cit., p. 3.
247 Ibid., p. 3.

Taylor's writings are full of exquisite phrases and prose of great beauty. He valued words highly and knew the classical writers better than any of his contemporaries. He was always quoting "those wise old spirits," as he called them. In his tract *The Faith and Patience of the Saints*, he has this passage which shows very well his particular beauty of thought and style:

Jesus was like the rainbow which God set in the clouds as a sacrament to confirm a promise and establish a grace. He was half made of the glories of the light and half of the moisture of a cloud; in his best days, he was but half triumph and half sorrow.[248]

It is in *The Great Exemplar* and *Holy Living and Holy Dying* that Taylor is at his greatest as a spiritual writer. *The Great Exemplar* is the first life of Christ written in English. Taylor's aim, like Andrewes's, was to help people become holy "by following after the most holy Jesus." *The Great Exemplar* was written for this purpose alone. It is interspersed with prayers and meditations, and as he treats of the events of the life of Christ he draws not a theological but a moral lesson. For instance, in his account of the Annunciation he says, "When the Eternal God stooped so low as to be fixed in our centre, he chose for his mother an holy person and a maid, teaching us [not a matter of theology or faith, but] that we hold forth no impure brands or smoking firebrands but pure and undimmed lamps in the eyes of the world."[249] The way to judge religion, he says, "is by doing our duty, and theology is rather a divine life than a divine knowledge." This imitation of Christ was to him religion, and religion meant the perfecting of human nature: "There is in Christianity and nowhere else enough to satisfy and inform his

---

248 Taylor, Sermon IV, "The Faith and Patience of the Saints," *Works*, vol. IV, p. 436.
249 Taylor, *The Great Exemplar*, vol. II, p. 53.

reason, to perfect his nature, and to reduce to act all the propositions of an intelligent and wise spirit."[250]

Two more passages from *The Great Exemplar* will give an impression of Taylor's warmth and sympathy. The first is about the Nativity in which Taylor pictures the Virgin touching each limb of her new-born son: "She kissed him and worshipped him, and thanked him that he would be born of her, and she suckled him and bound him in her arms."[251] The second is about the blessed Virgin also, but this time at the foot of the Cross: "By the cross of Christ stood the holy Virgin Mother upon whom old Symeon's prophecy was now verified . . . silent and with a modest grief, deep as the waters of the abyss, but smooth as the face of a pool . . . her hope drew a veil before her sorrow and though her grief was great enough to swallow her up, yet her love was greater and did swallow up her grief."[252]

Holy Living presents a sane and happy view of life which seems to echo the peace and order of Little Gidding. There are prayers and meditations woven in with the discussion of the virtues of the Christian life, and the last section contains prayers in preparation for communion. "Thou, O blessed Jesus, didst die for us; keep me ever in holy living . . . in the communion of thy church, and thy church in safety and grace, in truth and peace, unto thy second coming."[253]

Holy Dying was written in the period of grief following the death of Taylor's wife and of Lady Carbery. It is a long meditation on how to prepare for death. "In sickness," he says, "the soul begins to dress herself for immortality." It is in this work that he reveals his own feelings most clearly, and near the end is his comment on his own despair and sorrow: "Sometimes I have had some cheerful visitations of God's Spirit, and my cup hath been crowned with comfort and the

---

250 Ibid., Preface, p. 34.
251 Ibid., vol. I, III, pp. 66–7.
252 Ibid., vol. III, XV, p. 710.
253 Taylor, *Exercises for Holy Living*, *Works*, vol. III, IV, p. 253.

wine that made my heart glad danced in the chalice and I was glad that God would have me so; and I hope that this cloud may pass."[254]

Taylor's happy nature did not leave him long in despair, but it is a true and profound faith in God, rather than any natural feeling of felicity, that shines out in his works. He valued most of all a life ordered towards holiness and reflecting beauty, wonder, and delight in God. His sympathy and imagination, his kindness and understanding, made him one of the greatest of spiritual directors and devotional writers. But it is wise to balance the picture of Taylor's sweetness and joy with his griefs and trials: all his sons died in their youth, as well as his wife. This is a letter he wrote to John Evelyn which reveals him as a man and a saint: "Dear Sir, I am in some little disorder by reason of the death of a little child of mine, a boy that lately made us very glad, but now he rejoices in his little orb, while we think and long and sigh to be as safe as he is."[255]

Mark Frank (1613–1664)

The Anglican concern for sober piety and ordered loveliness is seen perhaps more clearly in the works of a less well-known divine, Mark Frank. His works consist of two books of sermons in which he can be seen as more representative of the ordinary Anglican divine of his day, although his prose style sets him in a place apart. Mark Frank was born in 1613, the same year as Jeremy Taylor. While Taylor was at All Souls, Oxford, under the patronage of Laud, Frank was scholar and later fellow of Pembroke College, Cambridge. He had to leave Cambridge because of his refusal to co-operate with the Protectorate, but he returned at the Restoration and was Master of Pembroke until he died in 1664 at the age of fifty-one.

254 Taylor, *Exercises for Holy Dying, Works*, vol. III, p. 432.
255 Taylor, Letter to John Evelyn, July 19, 1656, *Works*, vol. I, p. liii.

He was pre-eminently a scholar, preaching in a university setting; he was also a divine of the old High Church school, prepared to pay the price of his loyalty to the Church of England by losing his appointment under Cromwell. He was a friend and associate of Nicholas Ferrar at Little Gidding and presumably, therefore, of Ferrar's close friend at Cambridge, George Herbert.

Like Taylor, Frank was influenced by Andrewes; he refers to this fact in his third sermon on the Resurrection: "This is the day which the Lord hath made; this is the Lord's Day, of this day of the resurrection the Fathers of the Church and the Scriptures understand it. Not one of the Fathers, says the devout and learned Bishop Andrewes, that he had read (and he had read many) but interpret it of Easter Day."[256] Frank himself was in the tradition of the "witty" preachers in that he had a great regard for the meaning of words and would use every kind of figure of speech in his sermons. He had the command of words, the balance, contrast, and striking effect of Andrewes; the delicate observation of nature and the sympathy with mankind of Taylor; and he added to this his own grace of diction. His piety and simplicity turned his sermons into the old tradition of preaching in which the sermon was called *oratio*, the prayer.

In a sense, Frank stands between the elegant and highly wrought preaching of the turn of the century, and the plain moralistic sermons that came later. He breaks away from the use of conceits for their own sake and uses shorter sentences, simply welded together. Instead of finding meaning in every part of a text, he selects a theme—"Christ in rags," for example, for a Christmas sermon—and builds the sermon around it. His preaching is based on Scripture and theology, not on mere moralizing. He also avoids the tendency to pile text upon text, which was the bane of Puritan preaching. The best way to appreciate

256 Mark Frank, *Sermons*, Library of Anglo-Catholic Theology, 2 vols. (London, 1849), vol. II, p. 113.

Frank is to read his sermons; they are, unlike Andrewes's, immediately readable and convey, as they are set out, just what he meant to say. Some extracts follow:

Second Sermon for Christmas Day

Seeing the infinite greatness of this day become so little, Eternity a child, the rays of glory wrapped in rags, heaven crowded into the corner of a stable and he that is everywhere want a room . . . I am determined today to know nothing but Jesus Christ in a manger. He is wrapped up in poor cloths that we might be wrapped up in *stola prima*, the best robe, his robe of righteousness, that we might put on the white linen of the saints.

It is a day of mystery, it is a mysterious business we are about; Christ wrapped up, Christ in the sacrament, Christ in a mystery. Let us be content to let it go so, believe, admire and adore it.[257]

First Sermon on the Resurrection

Lose we Christ and we lose all our confidence in heaven, all the ways of access to heavenly things, all the pleasure and comfort of them; we are nothing but agues, and fears and frights; not courage enough even to look up. . . . But this is a day when perplexities cannot stay, fears cannot tarry with us, our heads cannot long hang down; at the rising of this day's Sun of Righteousness, our perplexities pass away as clouds before the sun; our tears melt as the dew before it; and we turn up our heads like flowers to the sunbeams. Angels fly everywhere about today, even into the grave, with comfortable messages. "Why weepest thou?" says one; "Fear not," says another; "Why

257 Ibid., vol. 1, p. 90.

seek you among the dead?" says a third. "What do you at the grave?" "He is risen," says the whole choir, he whose rising is all your risings, who is your Saviour now complete, and the lifter up of all your heads.[258]

Fourth Sermon for Whitsunday

Yet the business would be, how to catch this wind and serve our uses of it. Why, in the word and in the sacraments and by prayers we may have it and be filled with it. . . . Then the Spirit will descend upon our sacrifice and the wind of God's benediction upon our offering; and we shall return thence with mighty rushings in us, the rushing down of sin, the raising up of grace; mighty, mighty things will be done in us by the power of this Spirit and this wind; and as it came from heaven so thither it will back again and carry us upon its wings to keep a perpetual feast, an eternal Whitsunday all in white robes of everlasting glory. . . . Blow, O blessed wind, upon us this day; blow away our chaff and dross and dust out of our performances; breathe into thy holy mysteries the breath of a life-giving life; rush down all our sins before thee; purify and cleanse and refresh and revive and comfort us by thy saving breath that this wind may bring us good, all the good of heaven and earth; fill both our ears and our hearts here with sounds and songs of joy, and hereafter with alleluias for evermore.[259]

---

258 Ibid., vol. II, p. 88.
259 Ibid., vol. II, p. 255.

Sermon for St. Andrew's Day

Follow we St Andrew as he did Christ; follow him to Christ, cheerfully and without delay, and while it is today begin our course. Cast off but the net-works, the catching desires of the flesh and the world, and so you also may be said to have left your nets. And having so weaned your souls from inordinate affection to things below, let Christ be your business, his life your pattern, his commands your law. You may well throw away your nets, having caught him in whom you have caught glory and immortality and eternal life; and by following him shall undoubtedly come at last out of this sea of toil and misery into the port and haven of everlasting rest and joys and happiness.[260]

Sermon on the Annunciation

"*Dominus Tecum,*" the Lord Christ's being with Mary, is the chief business the Church especially commemorates in this day. Her being "blessed," and all our being "blessed," "highly favoured," or favoured at all, either men or women being so, all our hail, all our health, and peace, and joy, all the angels' visits to us, or kind words, all our conferences with heaven, all our titles and honours in heaven and earth, that are worth the naming, come only from it. For *Dominus Tecum* cannot come without them; he cannot come to us but we must be so, must be highly favoured in it, and blessed by it.

So the Incarnation of Christ, and the Annunciation of the blessed Virgin—his being incarnate of her, and her blessedness by him, all our blessedness in him with her, make

260 Ibid., vol. II, p. 392.

it as well our Lord's as our Lady's day. More his, because his being Lord made her a Lady, else a poor carpenter's wife, God knows; all her worthiness and honour, as all ours, is from him; and we take heed today, or any day, of parting them; or so remembering her, as to forget him; or so blessing her, as to take away any of our blessing him; any of his worship, to give to her. Let her blessedness the respect we give her, be "among women," still; such as is fit and proportionate to weak creatures, not due and proper only to the Creator, that *Dominus Tecum*, Christ in her be the business; that we take pattern by the Angel, to give her no more than is her due, yet to be sure to give her that, and particularly upon this day.

Blessed is the virgin soul, more blessed than others; blessed the humble spirit above all. For God hath exalted the humble and meek; none so happy, so blessed as she; the Lord comes to none so soon as such. Yet not to such at any time more fully than in the blessed Sacrament to which we are a-going. There he is strangely with us, highly favours us, exceedingly blesses us; there we are all made blessed Marys, and become mothers, sisters, and brothers of our Lord, whilst we hear this word, and conceive it in us; whilst we believe him who is the Word, and receive him too into us. There angels come to us on heavenly errands, and there our Lord indeed is with us, and we are blessed, and the angels hovering all about us to peep into those holy mysteries, think us so, call us so. There graces pour down in abundance on us; there grace is in its fullest plenty; there his highest favours are bestowed upon us; there we are filled with grace unless we hinder it, and shall hereafter in the strength of it be exalted into glory, there to sit down with this blessed Virgin and all the saints and angels, and sing praise and honour, and glory, to the Father, Son, and Holy Ghost, forever and ever.[261]

261 Ibid., vol. II, pp. 34ff.

9

PILGRIMAGE OF THE HEART
with Special Reference to
Lancelot Andrewes *and* John Bunyan

❖ ■ ❖ ■ ❖ ■ ❖ ■ ❖ ■ ❖ ■ ❖ ■ ❖

I take my title from a poem by George Herbert, entitled "Prayer":

Prayer the Churches banquet, Angels age

Gods breath in man returning to his birth,

The soul in paraphrase, heart in pilgrimage,

The Christian plummet sounding heav'n and earth . . .

Church-bels beyond the starres heard, the souls bloud,

The land of spices; something understood.[262]

I suggest that the "heart in pilgrimage" is the basic meaning of
Christian pilgrimages, whatever form they take, and that this inner
sense of pilgrimage is also a uniting element in human life. The *Oxford
Dictionary of the Christian Church,* however, has no such high-class
definition for pilgrimages; they are practical tours, mercenary even:
they are defined as "journeys to holy places undertaken from motives
of devotion in order to obtain supernatural help or as acts of penance
or thanksgiving."[263] These were indeed the motives uppermost in the
minds of the most famous of all pilgrims in Chaucer's *Canterbury
Tales,* and that is the usual picture that comes to mind when the word
is mentioned. It is in the spring that pilgrims set out:

262 George Herbert, "Prayer," *Poems of George Herbert* (Oxford, 1961), p. 44.
263 *Oxford Dictionary of the Christian Church,* ed. F. L. Cross and E. A. Livingstone
(Oxford, 1997).

Thanne longen folk to goon on pilgrimages

And palmerers for to seken straunge strondes

Of ferne halwes, kowthe in sondry londes,

And specially from every shires ende

In Engelond down to Canterbury they wende,

The hooly blisful martir for to seke

That hem hath holpen whan that they were seeke.[264]

The pilgrimage was a cheerful trip, in good company, with a definite place to go, with personal rewards in mind, for a limited season, with return home at the end of it. But even in Chaucer's day there were more serious challenges to the tourist version of pilgrimage; Langland, for instance, echoed later by Erasmus, took a severe view of "pilgrims and palmers full of clever talk," and for himself chose another kind of pilgrimage:

I swear by the Holy Rood of Lucca to devote all that is left of my life to the worship of Truth . . . and I will be His pilgrim, following the plough for poor men's sake.[265]

In fact, the idea of pilgrimage in the Christian Church has always been more than a temporary outing. It has provided an image of the inner life of Christians from the earliest times, and that inner strand was present still when the external reality of pilgrimage was emphasised as an increasingly popular form of devotion throughout the Middle Ages. The two concepts were not simple alternatives; they overlapped, and the several strands within each were constantly interwoven. There are ambiguities to be examined in these external and internal ideas of Christian pilgrimage.

264 Geoffrey Chaucer, *The Canterbury Tales*, in *Works of Geoffrey Chaucer* (Oxford, 1966), p. 17.
265 William Langland, *Piers the Plowman*, trans. J. F. Goodridge (Harmondsworth, 1959), p. 84.

The idea of pilgrimage as dispossession for the individual, as going away from earthly life towards heavenly life both in action and in idea, has a special reference to monasticism as a pattern for the Christian in the journey to the new Jerusalem. It remained as an implicit theme through the later practices of pilgrimage towards a shrine, which seemed to concentrate more on the idea of getting something earthly, whether healing or souvenirs or simply credit. The material side of such visits provoked stern rebuke in the sixteenth century when the idea of pilgrimage was given a new direction, more in line perhaps with the Letter to the Hebrews and the inner journey within the heart: "[They] confessed that they were strangers and pilgrims on the earth. For they that say such things declare plainly that they seek a country . . . that is, an heavenly [one]" (Heb. 11:13, 14, 16).

Inner and outer pilgrimage are not two clear and distinct concepts; in some ways what was outer for the Middle Ages is inner for us and vice versa. But within the framework of these two ideas it seems to me possible to disentangle at least five layers of meaning in the complex image of pilgrimage. Two of them are concerned with pilgrimage as detachment, as going out "away from"; two of them are concerned with longing and desire, with going "towards"; and one is concerned primarily with penance, something imposed rather than chosen. The first two were primarily a part of the inner pilgrimage of the heart by which those undertaking them returned to their homeland of heaven; the other three might be called mercenary pilgrimages, for simple gain of one kind or another. Clearly they overlap, but perhaps it will be useful to examine each in itself briefly.

Firstly, pilgrimage "from." This sense of detachment from self, from what is familiar, is the root meaning of *peregrination, per-agros:* to go through the fields, as a stranger, a foreigner, an outsider.[266] The

---

266 I am indebted to Professor Peter Brown for the idea of the outsider/*peregrinus,* especially in his seminal article "The Rise and Function of the Holy Man in Late Antiquity," *Journal of Roman Studies* LX1 (1971): pp. 80–101.

pilgrim is the outsider, one who has left his home, an exile who belongs nowhere. This idea of pilgrimage was frequently linked with Abraham going out from his own country, at the call of God: "By faith Abraham . . . went out not knowing whither he went . . . for he looked for a city which hath foundations and whose builder and maker is God" (Heb. 11:8, 10). The Gospels and Paul's Epistles are full of the call to all Christians to leave familiar ways and follow Christ. Early Christian monasticism showed this fundamental Christian calling in large poster-size images. Antony the Great—"before him no-one had sought the utter desert"—heard the Gospel read and followed it literally:

> he entered the church . . . and it so happened that the Gospel was being read and at that moment he heard the page in which the Lord says to the rich man, 'if you will be perfect, go, sell all that you have and give to the poor and come and follow me'; he left the church, gave away his property and devoted himself to living as a monk.[267]

It was a movement indeed, but detachment from domesticity was the motive, a going away from all that held back the heart from following Christ. This was true of the many others in the first days of the monastic movement; they left their homes absolutely to live in solitude, to undertake another inner pilgrimage. Some of them wandered from place to place, never settling for fear of becoming attached, and all of them were ready to move away if the place impeded their inner pilgrimage. One of them made himself walk round his village at night to test how detached he was from longing for it.[268] Such detachment, even in its extreme manifestations, was not in itself a guarantee of inner progress: for instance, there was a monk who decided to spend

---

267 Athanasius, *The Life of St Antony,* trans. Robert Mayer (London, 1950), pp. 19–20.
268 *Sayings of the Desert Fathers: The Alphabetical Collection,* trans. Benedicta Ward, SLG (Oxford/Kalamazoo, 1975/84/98), Poemen 110, p. 183.

his life in the total detachment of running with a pack of antelopes; he enjoyed it so much that one day he said to God, "Let me do something really hard for your sake"; and God told him to go into a monastery. A week later the monk said, "O God, let me go back to the antelopes."[269]

The Irish were especially expert at this sense of detachment and journeying: for instance, the three men in a boat without oars who came, says the *Anglo-Saxon Chronicle* for 891, to the court of Alfred, leaving home with no intention of returning, aiming for nowhere, were "on pilgrimage for the love of God, going they cared not where";[270] they were, as the author of the life of St. Guthlac put it, *viatore Christe*, travelling with Christ.[271] The fictional *Voyage of St Brendan* described another setting out in which it was better to travel hopefully than to arrive: "from time to time the wind filled their sails though they knew not whence it came or whither it was taking them."[272]

Secondly, this exile from home could lead to a new home, a new stability. The perpetual wanderer, a pilgrim in the first sense, could become the second kind of pilgrim; the exile from home who went out from his own place might then settle down in another place. The inner pilgrimage was continued but in a stable place. There could be conflict between the two ways: there is a story from Egypt of a recluse who lived alone for many years in her cell in Rome; she was visited by Sarapion, one of the more bizarre monks of Egypt who was— untypically—famous for wandering naked everywhere. He expressed, most unwisely, his indignation that she received credit from the townsfolk as a saint because she did nothing: "Why are you sitting here and doing nothing?" he asked her; and she replied, "I am not

---

269 *World of the Desert Fathers,* trans. Columba Stewart (Oxford, 1975).
270 *Anglo-Saxon Chronicle,* 891, ed. and trans. D Whitelock, in *English Historical Documents,* vol. 1, c. 500–1042 (Oxford, 1979), pp. 200–201.
271 *Felix's Life of St Guthlac of Crowland,* ed. and trans. Bertram Colgrave (Cambridge, 1956), xxv, p. 88.
272 "The Voyage of St Brendan," trans. J. F. Webb, in *The Age of Bede,* ed. David Farmer (Harmondsworth, 1965), p. 213.

doing nothing; I am on a journey."[273] The exile from home became a
traveller in his desire for God, travelling in stability. Free from self and
domesticity, the pilgrim placed himself in the hands of God, and that
could lead to any number of things. Columba, leaving Ireland, settled
on the Isle of Iona with, it must be admitted, many missionary visits
elsewhere, with a new and stable base, but away from Ireland:

> Delightful I think it to be in the bosom of an isle,
>
> on the peak of a rock,
>
> that I might often see the calm of the sea,
>
> that I might see its heavy waves over the glittering ocean,
>
> as they chant a melody to their Father in their eternal course.
>
> That I might see its ebb and its flood tide in their flow,
>
> that this might be my name a secret name
>
> 'He who turned his back upon Ireland'.[274]

The point is "freedom from" an ascetic attitude, and of course the
pilgrimage is an inner one in stability. This detachment from the narrow
shell of self by pilgrimage in body prompted the soul to allow what
Augustine called the healing of the eyes of the mind, so that earthly life
was also transfigured, and the eagerness for the final journey to heaven
became a passion:

> I wish O Son of the living God, ancient eternal king,
>
> for a secret hut in the wilderness
>
> that it may be my dwelling . . .
>
> a lovely church, decked with linen,

273 Palladius, *The Lausiac History,* trans. R. T. Meyer (London, 1965), no. 37,
      Serapion, pp. 108–9.
274 "St Columba's Island Hermitage," *A Celtic Miscellany,* trans. K. Hurlston
      (Jackson, Harmondsworth, 1951), p. 223.

a dwelling for the God of heaven;

then bright candles over the holy white scriptures.[275]

The monastic pilgrimage of going away from self, in order to travel towards that death which is life, stressed the inner motive of the heart in leaving all. But a third layer of pilgrimage saw pilgrimage more in terms of going towards an earthly goal and coming back again. The first two exile-pilgrimages could use as their underlying theme the great verses of the Epistle to the Philippians: "He emptied himself . . . and became obedient unto death for us" (Phil. 2:7, 8). The theology of dispossession, to live in union with God in Christ reconciling the world to himself, the *kenosis* of Christ the ground of salvation, underlies this monastic sense of pilgrimage in the early period of the Middle Ages. But in the eleventh century the emphasis shifted in two ways: both by re-affirming the inner pilgrimage of stability with a renewed interest in self-knowledge, but also by moving towards *sequela Christi*, following in the actual footsteps of the man of Galilee: "it was not until the twelfth century that the image of journeying became a popular expression of a spiritual quest."[276]

This was not new; since the fourth century Palestine had been the Holy Land, the earthly place to which pilgrims wanted to go. As Jerome said, "it is better to live for Jerusalem than to journey to Jerusalem,"[277] but there is the undoubted fact that he lived near Jerusalem himself and got there by going on the feet not of the heart but of the legs; it was there that he wished to live and discover the pilgrimage of the heart *nudus nudum christum sequi.*[278] He also admired and described the lengthy pilgrimage of his friend and companion the matron Paula to

---

275 "Wish of Manchan of Liath," in ibid., p. 223.
276 For a seminal discussion of this point, see R. W. Southern, *The Making of the Middle Ages* (London, 1953), chap. 5, "From Epic to Romance," pp. 209–45.
277 *The Principal Works of St Jerome,* vol.VI, trans. W. F. Freemantle (Grand Rapids, MI: Wm. B. Eerdmans, 1979), Letter LVIII, To Paulinus, p. 119.
278 Ibid., Letter CXXV, To Eustocium, p. 252.

Egypt and to Jerusalem.[279] Pilgrimage could mean actual mobility in the fourth as in the fourteenth century, not simply freeing oneself from familiar surroundings to seek the kingdom, but going "away from" in order to go towards a definite holy place on earth. The chief place of such pilgrimages has always been and still is Jerusalem. The great pilgrimages of the Crusades were inspired by love of the earthly place where Christ had lived and died. Though St. Paul had made it clear that it is "the Jerusalem which is above which is free" (Gal. 4:26) which is the aim and goal of the disciple, still the actual earthly location mattered. There are plenty of records of such pilgrimages, both to Palestine and to Egypt, beginning with the empress Helena and recorded of John Cassian and Germanus, Postumianus the admirer of Martin of Tours, and those enterprising women Paula, Melania, and Egeria. But in the eleventh century there was a new passion, a new emotion, a new desire to walk where Jesus of Nazareth had walked, to follow as his disciples had done. The Russian abbot Daniel and his companions who visited the Holy Sepulchre in the eleventh century came there in order to "see with our own eyes all the places that Christ our God had visited for our salvation."[280] Because of this historical presence on that particular piece of earth, the Holy Land was seen in a new light as one of the places where there was assurance of holiness, a chink through which one could be helped to slip more easily into heaven.

Jerusalem was not the only such place; Rome, the place of the martyrs, especially of the grave of St. Peter, ran it a close second. Where else could anyone find such assurance of help in the last days than there at the tomb of the chief of the apostles, the keeper of the keys of the kingdom? After about 900, the other place of distant pilgrimage was the tomb of the apostle James at Compostela in Spain. Sometimes

---

279 Ibid., Letter CVIII, To Eustocium, pp. 195–224.
280 *The Pilgrimage of the Russian Abbot Daniel to the Holy Land*, trans. C. M. Wilson (London, 1888), p. 405.

these goals of pilgrimage were places of permanent exile—some of the Anglo-Saxon kings went to Rome and stayed there to die. It is worth remembering the hazards of the long journeys and the possibility that, whatever one intended, one might not in fact return. But mostly pilgrims came back; it was a journey during which you were counted as a monk to some extent, but it would not involve permanent exile.

Fourthly, it was increasingly possible to go on pilgrimage towards a more local place—a place not entirely remote, the tomb of a local saint. These were the pilgrimages which were most carefully recorded and to which historians have turned their attention in the last fifty years or so. Many of the sick who could not go on a longer pilgrimage could go to their local shrine; sometimes when healed there they would then undertake the longer pilgrimage out of devotion. William of Wales, for instance, whose bent back had for two years prevented him from undertaking a pilgrimage to the Holy Land, came to the shrine of St. Frideswide in Oxford in the twelfth century: the saint "appeared to him, . . . and covered him with a white bear's skin . . . he sensed that he was cured . . . after a few days he set out with a healthy body on a journey to the Holy Sepulchre."[281]

The pilgrims visiting their local shrines wanted personal results and especially the sick came or were brought, in this last-ditch attempt to obtain a cure. This type of pilgrimage seems to have been the kind most easily deflected from the solemn matter of making oneself empty enough to receive God; it could become a way of going in order to get, with perhaps little effort involved. It also resulted in the business-sense of those living around the shrines being sharpened; they realised their assets with assiduous collecting of offerings.

The extreme of this came perhaps with pilgrimages made by the relics of saints themselves—for example, the journeys of the hairs of

---

281 *Miracula S. Frideswidae*, by Prior Philip, *Acta Sanctorum*, Oct. 8 no. 10, pp. 567–90.

the Virgin from Laôn in the twelfth century, primarily undertaken as a money-making expedition for church building.[282] It is not the carrying about of relics that is remarkable; there are many instances of relics being carried about personally by individuals, and of relics being taken in procession; what is striking here is the openly mercenary motive expressed. The cathedral of St. Mary at Laôn was damaged by fire in 1112, and Bishop Bartholomew launched a campaign to raise money to rebuild it. He sent some of his clergy on fund-raising tours, carrying the relics of the church, most notably the relic of the hairs of the Virgin Mary; "with us we took the feretory of Our Lady . . . to receive the offerings of the faithful." From Pentecost 1112 until September 21, they toured northern France, stopping in various towns so that the relics could be venerated and offerings made; the party returned with considerable funds, and next year from Palm Sunday 1113 the relics went on a second pilgrimage to the south of England, which was thought to be particularly prosperous. Canon Hermann who wrote the account made it clear that it was by no means an easy journey, and he recorded some remarkable adventures—for instance, among the Devon men who defended with their fists their right to own King Arthur against these foreigners, and with the slave traders in Bristol who nearly kidnapped the canons. But they returned home in September with a hundred and twenty marks; the pilgrimage of the relics was a financial success, though it is not easy to link it with the deeper concepts of peregrination.

All these four kinds of pilgrimage were voluntary, but fifthly there were the penitential pilgrimages, on which sinners could be sent as a penance for sin not by choice but by command. These began to be imposed in the sixth century and existed in Chaucer's day—the Parson says "whan a man hath synned openly . . . than hooly chirche

---

282 *De Miraculis S. Mariae Laudunensis*, PL 156, cols. 961–1020. (Also mentioned by Guibert of Niogent in his autobiography *De Vita Sua*.)

by juggement destreyneth hym for to do open penaunce . . . as for to goon peraventure naked in pilgrimages or barefoot."[283] The thirteenth century made Rome especially the place for absolution after Innocent III instituted indulgences to be gained by pilgrimage to Rome every fiftieth year, the years of jubilee. The three great shrines of Jerusalem, Rome, and Compostela were special places which offered absolution; they were the gates of heaven, the assured places of the patronage of the saints for sinners.

Notorious sins, especially public crimes of the great, were given public penance. Sometimes the penitent was told to wear chains on his journey; in one horrific instance a murderer was made to wear the corpse of the man he had murdered, having it fastened to his back all the way from Germany to Spain. Probably he was sent to St. James because "it is plain that whoever goes truly penitent to St. James and asks for his help with all his heart will certainly have all his sins blotted out."[284] A notorious sinner would need influential celestial patronage working for forgiveness, and so he would be sent to the places most closely associated with the greatest saints, whether a tomb or the place of a vision, or a relic, or just a church.

The distant penitential pilgrimage could even be imposed as a permanent way of life for a great crime. When Innocent III was approached with the story of Robert the Cannibal, he was strict indeed. Robert had been captured during a crusade with his wife and child; when released he confessed that as a captive of the Saracens he had been forced to kill, cook, and eat his infant daughter; he also obeyed orders to kill his wife, but had finally collapsed when asked to eat her too. The penance imposed by the pope included as one of its regulations that he should never sleep in the same place for the rest of his life but

283 Chaucer, The Parson's Tale, p. 229.
284 *Codex Calixtinus*, ed. Walter Muir Whitehill, 2 vols. (Compostela, 1944), Sermon *Veneranda Dies*, vol. 2, p. 144.

travel from one shrine to another, a permanent pilgrim.[285] In this case it was the pilgrimage itself that was absolution—which brings it very close to the permanent pilgrimage undertaken by the monk.

These kinds of pilgrimage were not exclusive. Pilgrimage undertaken for devotion could become a penitential pilgrimage, which in turn could become the monastic inner pilgrimage in stability. This is illustrated by the story of a German tanner who undertook a pilgrimage of devotion with companions to Compostela around 1100; there are at least eight versions of this popular story, but the version I quote was that told to Anselm of Canterbury by Hugh of Cluny, in the monastery of Cluny where the man concerned, Giraldus, ended his days as a monk.

> Giraldus made a vow to go on pilgrimage to St James of Compostela, but just before setting out he went to say goodbye to his mistress and his farewell kiss led to consummation of his lust . . . the devil suggested to him that he might as well end so sinful a life . . . Giraldus then cut off his own genitals and cut his throat with a knife. . . . Restored to his body by the prayers of St James, St Peter and the Virgin Mary, he completed his pilgrimage as a penance and then became a monk at Cluny.[286]

The story shows the more or less carefree approach of pilgrims at the beginning of a journey; the expectation, however, that such a journey would involve the monastic virtue of celibacy; and the conversion of the journey into the inner pilgrimage of the monk after an experience of death and judgement and the power of the intercession of the saints. In this case the secular pilgrim became the monastic pilgrim, but more usually among the dangers and delights

285 *Miracula S. Anselmi*, in *Memorials of St Anselm*, ed. R. W. Southern and F. C. Schmitt, *Auctores Britannici Medii Aevi* 1 (London, 1969), pp. 273–74.
286 Ibid.

of actual pilgrimage, it was easy to lose sight of any deeper concept. The practical matters of inns for lodging and company on the way, for instance, belonged to the secular world, not the religious one, and even with such a devout pilgrim as Paula, Jerome had expressed concern about pilgrimage involving her in such matters; he advised Paulinus not to go for just that reason.

Mixed in with the accounts of actual pilgrimages, there was always a thread of doubt, of warning, a desire to stress the basic idea of inner pilgrimage. Augustine, in the *City of God*, saw the Church on earth as made up of aliens, people without residence visas, the Church *in via,* in pilgrimage, and recommended not visits to shrines, but a lifelong journey of conversion of heart. For him, the inner pilgrimage, the theme of exile, continued into its resolution in heaven where "we shall rest and we shall see, we shall see and we shall love, we shall love and we shall praise, behold what shall be in the end without ending."[287] Bede, the most static and stable of men, hardly ever leaving his monastery at Jarrow, endorsed this concept of inner pilgrimage:

> The house of God which king Solomon built in Jerusalem is a symbol of the holy universal church, chosen from its beginning until its end . . . daily it is being built up in peace by the grace of the king . . . part of it is in pilgrimage here on earth, part has passed from this harsh pilgrimage and already reigns with him in heaven to wait there with him until the last day when all things shall be put under his feet. . . . This house is still on a journey, in order to come to the land of promise, yet it is being built in that land of promise in the city of Jerusalem; in the present time the church is in exile, in future it will be at home in peace.[288]

---

287 Augustine, *City of God,* trans. H. Bettenson, Bk. XXII, cap. 30, p. 1091.
288 Bede, *On the Temple,* trans. Sean Connolly (Liverpool, 1995), p. 5.

Anselm of Canterbury described the inner search for conformity of life to God as an ascent, a continual pilgrimage of life, concluding his *Proslogion* with longing for the end and goal of the journey:

> My God,
>
> I pray that I may so know you and love you
>
> that I may rejoice in you.
>
> And if I may not do so fully in this life
>
> let me go on steadily
>
> to the day when I come to that fullness.[289]

Bernard of Clairvaux, writing to Alexander of Lincoln about a canon who had gone on the pilgrimage called crusade, was even more explicit about the true place of the pilgrim when he says that this Philip has

> entered the holy city and has chosen his heritage . . . he is no longer an inquisitive onlooker but a devout inhabitant and an enrolled citizen of Jerusalem. . . . If you want to know this Jerusalem is Clairvaux. She is the Jerusalem united to the one in heaven by wholehearted devotion, by conformity of life, and by a certain spiritual affinity.[290]

But these monastic writers did not scorn actual pilgrimages: with their concentration on inner pilgrimage, there was a right place for actual pilgrimage; everyone has different needs at different times, and sometimes the inner journey would be helped by an outward one. The images of pilgrimage needed external manifestation at some point or the metaphor would not have any meaning, just as at some point there must be actual lovers or the images of the *Song of Songs* relating the

---

289 Anselm, *Proslogion* cap. 22, in *Prayers and Meditations,* p. 266.
290 *Letters of St Bernard of Clairvaux,* trans. Bruno Scott James (London, 1953), Letter 67, pp. 90–92.

soul to God have no inner meaning. So Augustine, Bede, Anselm, and Bernard all recommended actual pilgrimage, though always within the overriding purpose of the inner journey. In the twenty-second book of the *City of God*, Augustine expressed delight that Christians should come to visit the shrine of St. Stephen in Hippo. In his *Ecclesiastical History* Bede praised the Anglo-Saxon pilgrims to Rome; Anselm listened with interest to stories of pilgrimages, and Bernard sent more men to Jerusalem as crusader-pilgrims than perhaps any other preacher at any time.

The connection is not a simple one of a practical earthly journey contrasted with an inner spiritual journey. The overlap of actual pilgrimage and inner pilgrimage has four possibilities:

1. It was possible to stay and to stay, in other words to be completely lazy and attempt nothing, go nowhere, stay shut within the walls of self, to ignore pilgrimage altogether.

2. It was possible to stay and yet to go, by undertaking the pilgrimage of the heart while remaining in one place, which was the fundamental monastic way.

3. It was possible to go inwardly by longing and desire in the heart and to confirm this by outward pilgrimage with the feet, to be a true pilgrim.

4. It was possible to go on pilgrimage with feet but not with heart, as a tourist, a runaway, or a drop-out from responsibility, a curious inquirer, in which case there had been no real inner movement; the traveller had taken the shell of self with him, and whatever its name it was not in essence a pilgrimage at all.

It was the last of these, the mercenary pilgrimage, which attracted criticism from all sides in the sixteenth century. It is necessary here to refer to the fact that pilgrimage was linked to the veneration of saints, to the sense that those on earth were surrounded by a great cloud of witnesses, who could be reached, appealed to, who were alive and accessible, if unpredictable. Bede described this as the sixth age of life now in progress between the first and second coming of Christ, with the seventh age of the saints who are alive in Christ running parallel to the sixth age, both converging on the eighth age, the day of the Lord. Those in the seventh age could be reached and would aid those in the sixth *in hac lacrymarum valle,* and therefore to visit the places associated with them seemed right and natural.

But the reformers were critical of anything to do with the cult of saints; the sense of the household of heaven, of a great cloud of witnesses, always near, always accessible, which was the setting for medieval pilgrimage, was seen as an impediment to true knowledge of God and sternly rejected in favour of a simple, personal access to the Lord alone. Most obviously, veneration of and appeal to the saints led to pilgrimage to shrines in expectation of miracles and a desire for relics, and this could be seen to engender a greed for what Bonhoeffer has called "cheap grace." The criticisms of the Catholic Erasmus were as searing as those of the Protestant Calvin. Physical pilgrimage was derided and then rejected.

Yet it is in the ensuing centuries in the Protestant world that the ideal of inner pilgrimage flowered; not for nothing did I take the title of this chapter from a seventeenth-century Anglican poet. The outward trappings of pilgrimage were given a totally inner meaning as terms used to describe the life of any ordinary Christian. The severe reaction of the Reformation in the destruction of shrines and monasteries and the abolition of pilgrimages had the surprising result of popularising and interiorising the monastic concept of pilgrimage as never before. Pilgrimages had indeed become shockingly materialistic; they had to go; but the outward gear of pilgrimage provided the symbols of that inner devout life which led the new pilgrim to God. A poem which used to be attributed to the Elizabethan courtier and pirate Raleigh was based on such imagery:

> Give me my scallop-shell of quiet,
>
> My staff of faith to walk upon,
>
> My scrip of joy, immortal diet,
>
> My bottle of salvation,
>
> My gown of glory, hope's true gage,
>
> And thus I'll take my pilgrimage.[291]

What made a pilgrim was now not the scrip, the gown, the staff, or the shell of St. James, but travelling with Christ in a lifetime of leaving self and receiving him. Since the way into this new Jerusalem, the city of gold, had to be by a Cross and the river of death, the way of the pilgrim was not simple, light-hearted, or easy. The image of journeying was to provide also the interior theme of the two great Catholic mystical writers of the sixteenth century: with Teresa of Avila, the pilgrimage was through the many mansions of a house; with John of the Cross it was the ascent of a mountain where "the way there is the way back and the way up is the way down and where you are is where you are not." It may well be that this inner concentration without outward expression placed too great a burden on the individual; but it was meant as a way of freedom and life.

I will conclude by quoting two pieces of literature from that world of earnest inner pilgrimage, which show, I think, that the essence of pilgrimage is an inescapable image always and everywhere. Since

---

291 "The Passionate Man's Pilgrimage," in *The Oxford Book of 16th Century Verse*, chosen by E. K. Chambers (Oxford, 1932), p. 497.

pilgrimage belongs to everyone, regardless of class or position, clerical or lay, monastic or secular, rich or poor, I have been happy to be able to choose these passages from two men whose positions were in the sharpest possible contrast. The first is by a bishop of Winchester, a courtier, the most learned man of his day, a friend of kings and princes; the second is by a poor brazier of Bedford who taught himself to read the Bible and who lay in prison when he wrote. The first is a section from one of Bishop Lancelot Andrewes's sermons on the Nativity, preached before James I at Whitehall on Christmas Day 1622 on the paradigm pilgrimage in Matthew 2:1–2, "Behold, there came wise men from the east to Jerusalem." The other, from the finest piece of all English pilgrimage literature, forms the conclusion of John Bunyan's *Pilgrim's Progress,* in which the pilgrimage of life finds its real end in death and the gateway to the kingdom.

Andrewes began his sermon with his customary careful linguistic attention to the text, but concluded with an immediate application of the ideal for his hearers of coming to Christ, making the preliminary and to us surprising point that pilgrimage to Christ is not restricted to poor and ignorant shepherds:

> Christ is not only for russet cloaks, shepherds and such, shews Himself to none but such. But even the grandees, great states such as these, *venerunt,* 'they came' too; and when they came were welcome to him. For they were sent for and invited by this star, their star properly.

He continued by summarising his account of the pilgrimage of the Magi (to us reminiscent of the use of this, and a subsequent sermon, by T. S. Eliot):

Whence? From the East, their own country. Whither? to Jerusalem. . . . They came a long journey. . . . They came an uneasy journey, . . . And they came a dangerous journey, . . .

And they came now, at the worst season of the year. And all but to do worship at Christ's birth. . . . So desirous were they to come with the first, and to be there as soon as possibly they might; broke through all these difficulties, *Et ecce venerunt*, 'And, behold, come they did.' . . .

And these were wise men, and never a whit the less wise for so coming; nay never so truly wise in any thing they did, as in so coming.

The ideas of pilgrimage "from" and "towards" were both used here and were then given a new direction in which the inner pilgrimage was expressed in a new physical direction by an immediate application of the text to his hearers:

And how shall we that do? . . .

And in the old Ritual of the Church we find that on the cover of the canister, wherein was the Sacrament of His body, there was a star engraven, to shew us that now the star leads us thither, to His body there.

And what shall I say now, but according as St John saith, and the star, and the wise men say, 'Come.' And He, Whose the star is, and to Whom the wise men came, saith 'Come.' And let them that are disposed, 'Come.' And let whosoever will, take of the 'Bread of Life which came down from Heaven' this day into Bethlehem, the house of bread. Of which Bread the Church is this day the house, the true Bethlehem, and all the Bethlehem we have now left to come to for the Bread of life, . . . And this our

nearest coming that here we can come, till we shall by another
venite come, unto Him in His Heavenly Kingdom.[292]

This advice to make a pilgrimage to the altar, the house of bread, the
new Bethlehem, showed a near and practical way through life for the
Christian pilgrim; the inner pilgrimage could be helped by an outward
ascent. There was a practical going in order to continue the inner one.
But John Bunyan sounded a severer note in his account of the long
pilgrimage of life made by Christian and his companions from the City
of Destruction to the Valley of the Shadow of Death, through Vanity
Fair, past the Slough of Despond, Giant Despair, and so to the Celestial
City. As he guided Christian's wife, Christiana, on the way, Mr. Valiant-
for-Truth sang,

Who would true valour see

let him come hither

One here will constantly

follow the master;

theres no discouragment

shall make him once relent

his first avowed intent

to be a pilgrim.[293]

Through all the difficulties of the way, the images of pilgrimage were
meant to describe a pattern of inner progress in the Christian life—not
a visible journey of any kind—but the story is so entrancing that it
is easy to forget the stern reality conveyed. It is perhaps ironic that
while the problem with actual pilgrimage was the attraction of material
excitements, in a similar way the difficulty with this account of inner

292 *Ninety-Six Sermons by Lancelot Andrewes,* vol. 1 (Oxford, 1841), pp. 243–47.
293 John Bunyan, *Pilgrim's Progress* (London, 1890), pp. 365–66.

pilgrimage is that its serious inner purpose can be nearly obscured by the pleasure of its imagery. A passage at the end expresses the new way of pilgrimage and makes clear that, under all the striking images, the pilgrim's progress had been as a *viator christi*, as travelling through life with Christ:

> Then there came forth a summons for Mr. Stand-fast (this Mr. Stand-fast was he whom the pilgrims found upon his knees in the Enchanted Ground). When Mr. Stand-fast had thus set things in order, and the time being come for him to haste him away, he also went down to the river. Now there was a great calm at that time in the river; wherefore Mr. Stand-fast, when he was about half-way in, stood a while, and talked to his companions that had waited upon him thither.

This was not a river-crossing but a death, and Mr. Stand-fast's reflections on his pilgrimage were concerned only with his life of conversion of heart in a passage built up from biblical texts applied with personal relevance:

> And he said, 'This river has been a terror to many; yea, the thoughts of it have also frighted me; but now methinks I stand easy; I see myself now at the end of my journey; my toilsome days are ended. I am going to see that head which was crowned with thorns, and that face which was spit upon for me. . . . I have loved to hear my Lord spoken of; and wherever I have seen the print of His shoe in the earth, there I have coveted to set my foot too. His name has been to me as a civet-box; yea, sweeter than all perfumes. His voice to me has been most sweet, and His countenance I have more desired than they that have most desired the light of the sun. His Word I did use to gather for my

food, and for antidotes against my faintings. He has held me, and hath kept me from mine iniquities; yea, my steps hath He strengthened in His way.'

For Andrewes and Bunyan the pilgrimage of the Christian was life itself, the end indeed death, and the way the way of the Cross. "Let us go unto him therefore without the camp bearing his reproach, for here we have no continuing city but we seek one to come" (Heb. 13:13). That was the path of every Christian pilgrim, whether the way included actual walking or not. But however severe and demanding the life of pilgrimage might be, the end of the pilgrimage was delight, pleasure, wonder, and love.

Now while he was thus in discourse, his countenance changed, his strong man bowed under him; and, after he had said, 'Take me, for I come unto Thee!' he ceased to be seen of them.

But glorious it was to see how the open region was filled with horses and chariots, with trumpeters and pipers, with singers and players on stringed instruments, to welcome the pilgrims as they went up, and followed one another in at the beautiful gate of the City.[294]

The path of a pilgrim has always had its pleasures and joys not only at the end but also in the experiences of shared love and delight on the way. After Christian had let go of his burden of sin at the wicket gate, "he gave three leaps for joy and went on his way singing."[295] To recognise the seriousness of the undertaking of *peregrinatio* need not diminish the glory of the end, or prevent it from being reflected in the delights of the way itself. For any journey to be called a pilgrimage there has to be a serious element of going "away from" and "towards,"

294 Ibid., p. 383.
295 Ibid., p. 59.

but it means also a joyful sense of going out freely in good company
with shared aim, which is, perhaps, to find that place which is most of
all home:

> To an open house in the evening
>
> Home shall men come,
>
> To an older place than Eden
>
> And a taller town than Rome.
>
> To the end of the way of the wandering star,
>
> To the things that cannot be and that are,
>
> To the place where God was homeless
>
> And all men are at home.[296]

296 G. K. Chesterton, "The House of Christmas," *Collected Poems of G.K. Chesterton* (London, 1933), p. 140.

ACKNOWLEDGEMENTS/PERMISSIONS

❧ ▪ ❧

"The Spirituality of St. Cuthbert" was originally read at an interdisciplinary conference in Durham in July 1987 to mark the 1300th anniversary of St. Cuthbert's death, first published in *St Cuthbert, His Cult and His Community to AD 1200* (Woodbridge, Suffolk, UK: Boydell Press, 1989), and then published as a booklet by SLG Press of Oxford, UK, in 1992.

"Bede and the Conversion of the Anglo-Saxons" was first published in *Word and Spirit: A Monastic Review*, no. 7, 1985 (Petersham, MA: St. Bede's Publications), 35–46.

"Bede and the Psalter" was originally read as The Jarrow Lecture at St. Paul's Church, Jarrow, in 1991 and then published as a booklet by SLG Press in 2002.

"Anselm of Canterbury: A Monastic Scholar" was first published as a booklet by SLG Press in 1973.

"Twelfth-Century English Hermits" was originally published as "The Relationship between Hermits and Communities in the West" in *Solitude and Communion: Papers on the Hermit Life*, ed. A. M. Allchin, by SLG Press in 1977.

"Three Preachers: Lancelot Andrewes, Jeremy Taylor, Mark Frank" was first published in *The Beauty of Holiness: An Introduction to Six Seventeenth-Century Anglican Writers* by SLG Press in 1976.

"The Pilgrimage of the Heart, with Special Reference to Lancelot Andrewes and John Bunyan" was first published by SLG Press in 2001.

ABOUT PARACLETE PRESS

WHO WE ARE

As the publishing arm of the Community of Jesus, Paraclete Press presents a full expression of Christian belief and practice—from Catholic to Evangelical, from Protestant to Orthodox, reflecting the ecumenical charism of the Community and its dedication to sacred music, the fine arts, and the written word. We publish books, recordings, sheet music, and DVDs that nourish the vibrant life of the church and its people.

WHAT WE ARE DOING

Books

PARACLETE PRESS BOOKS show the richness and depth of what it means to be Christian. While Benedictine spirituality is at the heart of who we are and all that we do, our books reflect the Christian experience across many cultures, time periods, and houses of worship.

We have many series, including *Paraclete Essentials; Paraclete Fiction; Paraclete Giants*; and the new *The Essentials of...*, devoted to Christian classics. Others include *Voices from the Monastery* (men and women monastics writing about living a spiritual life today), *Active Prayer*, the award-winning *Paraclete Poetry*, and new for young readers: *The Pope's Cat*. We also specialize in gift books for children on the occasions of Baptism and First Communion, as well as other important times in a child's life, and books that bring creativity and liveliness to any adult spiritual life.

The MOUNT TABOR BOOKS series focuses on the arts and literature as well as liturgical worship and spirituality; it was created in conjunction with the Mount Tabor Ecumenical Centre for Art and Spirituality in Barga, Italy.

Music

The PARACLETE RECORDINGS label represents the internationally acclaimed choir *Gloriæ Dei Cantores*, the *Gloriæ Dei Cantores Schola*, and the other instrumental artists of the *Arts Empowering Life Foundation*.

Paraclete Press is the exclusive North American distributor for the Gregorian chant recordings from St. Peter's Abbey in Solesmes, France. Paraclete also carries all of the Solesmes chant publications for Mass and the Divine Office, as well as their academic research publications.

In addition, PARACLETE PRESS SHEET MUSIC publishes the work of today's finest composers of sacred choral music, annually reviewing over 1,000 works and releasing between 40 and 60 works for both choir and organ.

Video

Our DVDs offer spiritual help, healing, and biblical guidance for a broad range of life issues including grief and loss, marriage, forgiveness, facing death, understanding suicide, bullying, addictions, Alzheimer's, and Christian formation.

SCAN
TO
READ
MORE

Learn more about us at our website:
www.paracletepress.com or phone us toll-free at 1.800.451.5006